A WAY IN A MANGER

Christmas. What's all the fuss

Mark Hill

*To my wife Suzanne and children Joseph, Lily Mae
and Isaac
1 John 4:19; We love because He first loved us.*

ACKNOWLEDGEMENT

To Dave & Karen Johnson
who encouraged me to get writing.

Cover Photo by Walter Chavez on Unsplash

Lily Mae thank you for your guidance on the cover

Unless otherwise stated all Bible quotations
are from the New Living Translation

CONTENTS

INTRODUCTION

I have two sisters and lots of cousins. We enjoyed a great childhood, and each year was topped off with having a simply wonderful Christmas time. Charles Dickens would have been proud of the way we kept Christmas!

Our dad had a barber shop in West Bridgeford, then worked at Cottons a factory in Loughborough, then at the Brush all during our childhood. However, every Saturday he would stand on Loughborough market selling shoes. His older brother had shoe shops and if any were below par for the shop, they ended up on the market stall. Prospective customers were told if stitching was on the outside rather than inside or if one pair was made up of a size seven and a size eight. If they were happy with that the sale was made. For years I grew up thinking everyone had one foot shorter than the other. Next to dad's stall was Eric. He sold plants and shrubs. So, at Christmas we always had a real tree from him. Under the tree on Christmas Eve, we would leave a glass of milk and a mince pie for Santa, Rudolph the red nosed reindeer would get a carrot. I'm not sure why we didn't feed Dancer, Prancer, Blitzen, and the rest. Next morning, we would check early to see if the milk had been drunk, the pie had been eaten and if the carrot was gone.

They were and a note was always left. Thank you for the milk, mince pie and carrot, Love Santa. That was until that fateful Christmas day morning. The glass was empty, there were crumbs on the plate, the carrot was gone. The note read: Thank you for the milk, mince pie and carrot, Love Dad.

Love Dad? What? Why had Dad written the note? We always knew Dad and Santa had the same handwriting but now it seems Dad is signing it. Being the older brother, I distracted my sisters from what they really didn't understand anyway. However, for me, things were changing. What was this Christmas stuff all about? It deserved some investigating. As the magic of Christmas dissipated under the confusion of Santa's probable non-existence, it was still celebrated by everyone else. Everything carried on as before. Even the Queen didn't seem to know anything was wrong and broadcast her speech as if nothing had happened.

It was that same year we heard Slade sing "Merry Christmas Everyone" for the very first time ever. They fought for the top spot with Wizard and their "I Wish It Could Be Christmas Every Day". Every year since, for a couple of months before the event, they remind me of that day when I realised Christmas was not all it was supposed to be.

So, what is it then? After all it is a huge event. Retailers rely on it. Pop stars sing about it. Turkeys fear it and pine trees are torn down for it. It is a lovely time for some, for others it's a depressing disaster. Has commerce kept it going or is there more to it than we realise? Those two words, "Love, Dad", made me want to find out more.

1. IT'S TOO SOON.

We have hardly said goodbye to the summer. It will be some time before we put the clocks back an hour and yet, a couple of shelves in the supermarket already have upon them what we can only call, Christmas items. They call it the "Seasonal aisle", but we know what they are up to. The season is still summer, and the barbeques have made way for things that are wintery. Now we must hold our breath and wait with gritted teeth for the winter music to start. We will listen to it as we shop wearing shorts and T-shirts, dressed for the beach due to the fine English hot sunny weather. Because it is still summer!

I am pretty sure when I was younger Christmas only started a couple of weeks before the day. In my mind's eye, which might be a false nostalgic memory, there were no Carol Singers at least until there was snow on the ground, which there always was, at least the way I remember it! The Nativity play at school had to be rehearsed and then performed at the end of the school term, not the middle of summer. Decorations didn't go up in the house until a few days before the day. Santa was only visited in the big shop a week before he was due to call at the house. Maybe my memory is incorrect, but something has changed. Something has taken over from whatever Christmas used to be and made it into a commercial juggernaut that cannot be stopped. As a person who has faith in Jesus Christ, I would wish it was all about the historical event of Christ's birth, sadly it isn't. Perhaps it never was and maybe, according to some, it never should have been. Some, only a few, think it should not be celebrated at all.

Whatever else you think about it, Christmas is huge. Some Christians debate if there should be any involvement by believers in the celebrations. Some make a distinction between celebrating at home and not mentioning a thing about it in the confines of the church building. Some do it for the sake of the kids, after all your son really does need that Scalextric, (or is that dated now?). Other people who are not of faith celebrate hard going to parties and engaging in behaviour they might not get away with at any other time of the year. Having not attended church all year many call into a service on the way to the pub, as it is all part of the tradition, it is what you do at that time of year.

It might mean different things to different people, but it is a colossal event. There must be more to it than meets the eye. Whatever it has become, it started at some place and time. Perhaps it was "Away in a manger" in a "Little town of Bethlehem". How did Christmas get from there to Lapland? Truth has become mistaken for fiction and fiction has been repeated so often it is now confused with the truth.

If nativity plays, Christmas trees, reindeers, elves, mince pies and mistletoe are what it is all about what has the baby Jesus got to do with it at all?

Singers plan from July to get the Christmas number one. Film stars plan way ahead for a Christmas release to make the most of their film. A television talent show for the past few years in the UK has concluded in time for its winner to be in with a chance of getting the top slot. Television and radio programmes have Christmas specials. Theatres are given over to Pantomimes for a few weeks. Businesses pull out all the stops to increase and make the most of sales. Charities advertise themselves more and hope to see an increase in people's generosity because it is that time of year. Service providers might get a tip when there isn't even a thank you at any other time. Not only do children have parties at schools and clubs, but adults also enjoy office parties and bonuses. Even I am trying to get this book finished before the Boxing Day sales! Although they start the week before Christmas now, so I'm in with a chance.

There are of course some people who cannot get enough of Christmas and start preparing for it several weeks ahead. Others, personified by Dicken's creation of Scrooge, think the whole thing is a humbug and should be done away with. When you think how long ago that was written about the two opposing views over Christmas have been around for a long time. Why is there so much fuss? Isn't there enough going on in our lives and even on the world scene to occupy us? Is it only about commercialism? Do the dark cold winter nights emphasise our need of something, we are not sure what, but something to help make life a little more bearable? Maybe it does offer some kind of hope. Perhaps there is something behind it of such enormous implication it just cannot be denied?

Sin was and is a major problem in our world. We need a Saviour to rescue us from it. To provide salvation God came to us born as a baby to eventually do what was needed to save us from the punishment of our sin. God became human. This was a huge event the world has never been the same since it occurred. Of course, I know for a lot of the pop stars, businesspeople and charities doing what they do at Christmas time has no real connection with or thought of that. Yet, there is so much activity at that time of year surrounding the event, however loosely, that it leads us to believe a major event in history must have taken place.

We cannot blame it all on Charles Dickens, he wasn't the first to think of it. He shaped a lot of what happens now with a little help from Albert and Victoria and a few others of the era. The idea of a Victorian Christmas is still very popular and conjures up that "Christmassy feeling" as my daughter once called it. Over the years it has taken many forms and introduced characters that have nothing to do with the biblical account of Christ's birth.

A way was needed for us created humans to be reconciled with our creator. A way in a manger was opened having been promised and prophesied many years before. Christmas as we know it has little to do with the actual birth of Christ. However, it does in some way point to the most remarkable event in the world's history.

2. YOU BETTER WATCH OUT!

"You better watch out, you had better not cry, you better not pout I'm telling you why, Santa Claus is coming to town. He sees you when you're sleeping, he knows when you're awake. He knows if you've been bad or good, so be good for goodness' sake."[1]

What a frightening song to help you look forward to Christmas! Santa's naughty and nice list has been very useful to parents for many years. We can use it to get our children to behave at least for a few weeks leading up to December 25th. It is quite a creepy song if you think about it too much, after all who wants to be watched while they're sleeping. I romantically sang to Suzanne, my wife, the words of a song which says, "I could lay awake just to watch you sleeping" her response was to call me a weirdo.

The idea that "Santa Claus is coming to town", is used to encourage children to tidy their room otherwise Santa won't come. Children must put their toys away or Santa won't come with any presents. If they do not clear away their plates and cups at mealtimes, Santa will just fly past to give the presents to the good children.

Sadly, the words "Santa Claus is coming to town",

could well be a commentary on the way many people look upon and think about God.

When you picture God, who do you see? Like some, do you think of him as an elderly bearded man, living in a land far, far away. Santa Clause is someone we only think about at Christmas, could that be true of how often we think of Jesus too? Thoughts of Christmas though, these days, begin around October, is Jesus on the radar of our thoughts for that long? Is it really the case that God will only be nice to people who believe in him? Who can blame people for not wanting a god like that? But having faith in the God of all creation, the one revealed to us in the pages of the Bible, is very different from believing in Santa.

Many people that I know, like me, surrendered their life to Christ and were immersed in their teenage years. It often seems though, that what was good and appropriate when we were in our teens gets left behind with our childish toys as now inappropriate. There are things that we grow out of, and it is right and proper that we do.

Most often nowadays adolescents leave home to go to university. Now there is a need to make decisions for yourself. Advice is always available but with freedom comes personal responsibility. It is at this time that many who have been used to being part of a church family find they are in a place where there is not a congregation to easily get to. Getting out of the habit of meeting with a church, it becomes less convenient as other things seem to become more important. In the face of all the grown-up stuff the church seems less relevant. Sometimes the ordinary process of becoming an adult and getting caught up with grown up things distracts us. Work and career become our focus, because we think life will be so much better or easier if we earn that little bit more. I can't help but think about Robin Williams as Peter Pan in Hook. He is grown up now with grown up responsibilities, needing to take that vital business call rather than be in the moment with his family. Relationships begin and can be wonderful, but for some there is a harsh reality of discovering how awful some human beings can be towards others. Especially those they are supposed to love. If we think God is attached to Santa, then yes, the things of childhood get left behind. Santa cannot help with the terrible thing's life throws at us, except to help us with a bit of escapism once a year. What use is a God we picture as some kind of Santa Claus? It begs the question, "Do religious people only behave well because they want to go to heaven?" By being goodwill God treat us to a nice life, one where horrible things do not happen to us. A childish thought that doesn't seem to have been left behind with the other childish things. Why can't people just "be good for goodness' sake" and not because of the promise of divine reward or threat of terrible punishment?

This is a fair point. If religious people only behave well so they can earn a place in heaven that surely makes God just like Santa? In that case it is like telling children to behave so they'll get their presents at Christmas. God is having to put together a naughty or nice list and those on the nice list will get into heaven. For those who are not there will be separation from God. Is God really watching everything you do like some heavenly policeman waiting to catch you out? Does God have a ledger in which He calculates the number of naughty things you do against those nice things to balance the books. Will you be able to just scrape into heaven with one more act of kindness? In a word, no! In two words, certainly not!

According to the Bible there is nothing we can do to earn our place in heaven. What good deed makes up for a lie or gossip? What community service could make up for a burst of anger? Is there a one-off act of kindness that will compensate for the horrific acts of violence and abuse that are so much part of our society? Heaven is too far away from us because of our sin to be able to reach it. We can only get there because of what Jesus did on the cross. Being right with God is about admitting that nothing we can ever do will ever be good enough. But note also, there is nothing you have done that is so bad that God is not ready and able to forgive you. The Bible says that even the naughtiest of people can get on the "nice list" as it were and be with God forever. What counts is turning to him and away from what the Bible defines as sin. You cannot do enough, only Jesus is enough. The "naughty list", everything we have ever said, done or thought that is sinful in the eyes of God can be put to death as the Bible describes it, and you can start again, begin your life anew. To be born again means to start completely fresh. Our good deeds, once we have been immersed into Christ, are not a way of getting into heaven, they are a response from a thankful heart for what God has done.

This is not like visiting grandpa occasionally or that bearded old man who lives far away. It is turning towards, and spending the rest of your life with, God who has shown His love by coming to be amongst us. Sadly, Jesus coming to be with us is something that many will only celebrate or give a passing thought to at Christmas or maybe Easter.

A result of realising all that God has done for us gives cause to want to live in a way that is pleasing to Him. Being good is of course to be encouraged, what does it mean to be good? If human life is just an unlikely fluke in an otherwise random universe, where does our sense of right and wrong come from? Why should we believe there are some ways of behaviour that are better or more acceptable than other behaviours? What difference does it make if we are naughty or nice?

Someone who doesn't believe in God might say it's just obvious that we should be kind to others, treat people equally and make a difference for good. The problem is that it isn't obvious to everyone. Dictator's, abusers, and bullies seem to have no moral compass. Why can't they see what's plain for us to see? That they need to be good. But then, who decides what is good? To claim that they are wrong is to claim that there is a right way for the world to behave. And if they don't who are we to tell them that they're wrong? They would also have every right to just turn around and say our worldview is wrong?

To claim that some ways of living life are better than others there must exist a standard outside of us. What does a good life look like? How do we determine the standard out there in a random, purposeless universe? If there is a God who made us, it follows that the belief that there is a way that life should be lived makes perfect sense. The creator must have created for a purpose. It is reasonable to believe there is a reason for our existence. You know of course that something cannot come from nothing. If nothing ever existed there would still be nothing now. So, something has always existed. We have two options, therefore. What has always existed must be unintelligent matter, or a being with a mind. I will not insult your intelligence by pointing out that for obvious reasons we could not be the product of unintelligent matter. Common sense tells us that a mind must have always existed as everything around us came from a mind. Logic tells us there cannot be lots of God's. Therefore, there is one creator over us all.

Belief in Santa is something we grow out of but trusting in God is something we can continually grow into as we learn to appreciate just how good he really is. Science, common sense, logic, and philosophy tell us He is a supreme being, nothing like Santa. He is the same God who showed us His unlimited love in Jesus Christ. God has told us all about himself in the Bible and even lived amongst His creation by being born to Mary in Bethlehem.

Why is there so much fuss at Christmas? I suggest it has less to do with the day Jesus was born and more to do with the fact that there was a reason he was born when he was, in the place he was at the time he was. God wants us to know Him. Whilst who He is means he deserves our respect and adoration; He came so we would not need to "Watch out". He came to a manger in Bethlehem to provide a way for us to be with Him forever. His life demonstrated what it means to be good and how difficult it is for us to achieve it. Even so, He makes up for what we are unable to do. He provides forgiveness for sin in our life. He brought a way for us to find peace, a way to give us hope, a way for us to discover what it means to be loved and be able to love. No need to watch out, no need to cry and no pouting for sure. When Jesus came to town it was all part of a plan to provide us with a way to Him.

----

1 Santa Claus is Coming to Town" written by J. Fred Coots and Haven Gillespie in 1934

3. BEFORE AND AFTER

No matter how much people want to deny the existence of God, they cannot overcome the fact of the before and after. There was the world before Christ came and the world after he had been. For all the concerns people have about commercialisation and sickly films, come December it will be in your face again. Time will be given, around the world to celebrate in some way the birth of Christ. How odd that this is done by many who give no thought to God, Jesus, or the church throughout the rest of the year. On the other hand, there are some Christians who to distance themselves from all that might not be right about today's Christmas celebrations, end up throwing the baby Jesus out with the bath water. Seeing as there is not a direct command to celebrate Jesus' birth, many Christians try to avoid association with it or even mention it for fear of doing the wrong thing. Great effort is made to avoid saying Happy Christmas by offering "season's greetings" instead. What season would that be exactly? How ironic. Non-believers get involved in fully celebrating something they don't think happened, while believers if they celebrate at all, engage half-heartedly in a roundabout kind of way something they know did happen.

Christ's birth was a remarkable event in the history of the world. Jesus of Nazareth was born and lived on earth to do what was needed to be our Saviour. There is enough documented evidence for the existence of Jesus as an historical character as other historical characters whose existence we never question. There is no excuse on that basis to deny him. That people ignore Him the rest of the year and use Him as an excuse for celebrations, or to treat their children speaks volumes of the historical fact. We don't know the exact date in the year, and it is quite likely that he wasn't born right at year one. However, this is a remarkable event rooted in history and should not be ignored.

Reflect for a few moments on the fact that the birth of Jesus took place at a very precise moment in a particular place. The apostle Paul writes in Galatians chapter four verse four, *"But when the fullness of time had come, God sent forth His Son, born of woman..."* God Himself determined the exact moment in history when everything was ready for the birth of the Messiah. His birth had been promised and prophesied many years earlier. The protection of that promise being fulfilled is an adventure story told throughout the Old Testament the first thirty-nine books of the Bible. Why was Christ born in such a strange time and in such an out of the way place? It is a mystery to our modern minds. Neither Israel nor the rest of the world had the ability for global communication as we do today. Now we have twenty-four-hour, seven days a week news stations which all report events instantly because of the internet and mobile phones. At the time of Jesus birth there was no internet, no World Service, gossip columns, press, no radio, no smart phones, no daytime television to discuss a virgin birth or interview the shepherds. No social media or any kind of instant messaging. If it were me, I would have waited till now. If Christ had been born in our modern age, He could instantly have reached the whole world via "live" interviews on television. Instead, some shepherds had to nip into town and let people know. Today Jesus could have been an Instagram sensation, a real influencer, surely now would have been a better time to be born, especially if you wanted to get the news out. An appearance on, "I'm a Saviour Get Me Out of Here" would instantly provide Him with an opportunity to reach millions.

In view of all that, it seems a strange time for a world-wide Redeemer to be born. As well as global communication being easier, wouldn't now be a more opportune moment in history the way things are? After all, aren't we starved of good leadership not only at home but around the world. As far as the world stage is concerned which political leader would you prefer to be living under now? Surely there is a leadership vacuum to be filled. Right now, there is more global readiness to receive a new leader to come in and sort everything out, isn't there? Oh dear, listen to me. I sound like the people of Jesus' day who wanted a knight in shining armour to ride in and deliver them from the Romans. Perhaps nothing much has changed as far as the world being ready for Him is concerned. Who is really going to care about a king born in obscure circumstances and in a remote place without the benefit of world power and the modern media? Yet, as we read Scripture it demonstrates that according to God's Word the Messiah was to be born at a carefully determined time. A time that was right for God's way.

The apostle Paul in his letter to the Galatians uses the expression, "the fullness of time." The word fullness indicates that the preceding time has come to its fulfilment. Everything is ready, and therefore, according to God's wise direction, the birth can no longer be postponed. The time has come. The expression, "fullness of time" suggests that a certain period, characterised by constant preparation, has finally come to its conclusion. At the same time, it means that a new era has begun! The birth of Christ marks the close of an era and the beginning of a new period in the history of the world.

The words, "when the fullness of time had come," make clear that history can be divided into two specific periods. These periods are different, yet related. One is a time of preparation, while the other is a time of fulfilment. The one period cannot stand on its own but seeks its fulfilment in the other. Christ was born when all preparations had been made and when, according to God's plan, the conditions were perfect. From this expression, "the fullness of time," we learn that the birth of Christ propels the whole world into a new era. Christ's birth is a decisive event. Everything was moving towards this event and this event now determines all that still follows in the history of the world. The world we live in today is affected by that event.

Whatever you think about Christmas and all the toing and froing and pantomimes and food and office parties that go along with it. Whatever you think about all that. And whatever you think about it not being something authorised in scripture to remember or celebrate. It floods the shops, the restaurants, the night clubs the television and radio schedules, the cinema, and theatres and television ads. It is all around us and cannot be ignored. We could be forgiven for concluding that this annual, unstoppable event which seems to begin at the end of the summer holidays and is finally celebrated at the end of December, is the central event in the history of the world. Not tinsel and turkey Christmas of course but the birth of the Saviour of the world. God was guiding all things towards this birth as a focal point. All previous history makes sense only when seen in this light. Time had only one purpose: to come to its fullness, to the moment when the Messiah would be born.

The foolishness of believing in a big bang or Darwin's evolution or Dawkins's delusion is that no one knows what happened before those theoretical events nor what they are leading to. Self-important comedians mock it but offer no viable alternative, just anything for a laugh at the expense of believers.

Modern day scientists, if they can rightly be called scientists write books supporting evolution but ignoring scientific laws that do not allow for it. What was the purpose? Where are we heading to having had time started. The clock is ticking, but towards what? All world events only make sense when seen as being connected to this birth. Whereas the time before Christ's birth was focused on that very birth. The time after Christ's birth is focused on His return. We use the term Christmas because that speaks of all the stuff that happens now because of it. However, Christ is the centre of history. Without Him, time has no real meaning or function. He binds the ages together and moulds them into a unity. Therefore, all of time must be measured and appreciated with the birth of Jesus Christ at the centre. Take away the birth of Christ, and time becomes fragmented, disjointed, without any cohesion or direction. In much the same way if you take Christ out of your life, it, too, becomes meaningless. A series of events in a purposeless life leading to a meaningless death. Maybe the reason why Christ was born in a time without "mass communication" is that so often it is used to mislead people. Television is a deceptive medium with each company struggling to be unbiased. Social media is a platform for fake news and deception, it only gives fragments of what is really happening.

Do you get a little jealous when you see a picture posted of someone enjoying breakfast as they watch the sunrise with their feet up on the porch. They are so relaxed and obviously have time to think and contemplate the day. The picture you do not see is the one that could be taken five minutes later. In it you will see them battling to get the kids out of bed to go to school. This must be done in time for the parent to get to work themselves so they can be finished on time to pick the kids up later. When you see a snapshot, you do not get the whole picture. God's Word gives us the whole picture. Many people may celebrate Christmas in some traditional way with presents, turkey, mince pies, presents and Christmas films, but lose sight of the enormity of the event of Christ's birth. Often "Christmas" overshadows the scriptural account of an actual event. It gets isolated from its true context as a central fact in the history of the world. We do not doubt that the Romans ruled the world at the time or that their king ordered a census. In the birth of Christ there is a fulfilment of prophecies from previous ages and a decisive step towards the end of all the ages. "Christmas" is then either celebrated or avoided as merely a nostalgic tradition. What there must be, is a recognition of the central event in the history of redemption and therefore the history of the world. I'm not calling for a celebration or not of "Christmas" I am saying do not forget the truth that God was born into humanity at a particular time and in a particular place. What the season has become must not take away from the historical fact.

At Christmas time, many people only look back for a few moments to what happened once in Royal

David's city, that little town of Bethlehem, away in a manger to reflect on some shepherds watching their flocks by night, interrupted by some angels shouting Hark, Christ the Saviour is born. Nostalgia prevails. But in looking back surely, we are called to then look forward. The "fullness of time" directs us to the perfection of time, when the second period of history is completed with the return of Christ.

You see the period before Christ's birth was all about preparation. Now, our present, the time after Christ's birth is still all about preparation. Everything that happens in the world today has only one goal and purpose: being prepared for the return of the Lord. He who first came in deep humiliation, will return with heavenly majesty. On that day, time will be perfected, that is, it will have perfectly reached its goal. The redeemed will finally go home with the Lord. (Revelation 21:3-4): *"And I heard a loud voice from the throne saying, "Behold, the dwelling place of God is with man. He will dwell with them, and they will be his people, and God himself will be with them as their God. He will wipe away every tear from their eyes, and death shall be no more, neither shall there be mourning, nor crying, nor pain anymore, for the former things have passed away.""*

I am confident there was a before and after. Each time we write the date we point to the time Christ was born. I always thought that B.C. stands for "Before Christ" and A.D. stands for "after death." This is only half correct. How could the year 1 B.C. have been "before Christ" and A.D. 1 been "after death"? B.C. does stand for "before Christ." A.D. stands for the Latin phrase anno domini, which means "in the year of our Lord." The B.C./A.D. dating system is not taught in the Bible. It was not fully implemented and accepted until several centuries after Jesus' death. It is interesting to note that the purpose of the B.C./A.D. dating system was to make the birth of Jesus Christ the dividing point of world history. However, when the B.C./A.D. system was being calculated, they, the people involved in this, made a mistake in pinpointing the year of Jesus' birth. Scholars later discovered that Jesus was born around 6—4 B.C., not A.D. 1. That is not the crucial issue. The birth, life, ministry, death, and resurrection of Christ are the "turning points" in world history. It is fitting, therefore, that Jesus Christ is the separation of "old" and "new." B.C. was "before Christ," and since His birth, we have been living "in the year of our Lord." Viewing our era as "the year of our Lord" is appropriate. Philippians 2:10–11 says, *"That at the name of Jesus every knee should bow, in heaven and on earth and under the earth, and every tongue confess that Jesus Christ is Lord, to the glory of God the Father."*

In recent times, there has been a push to replace the B.C. and A.D. labels with B.C.E and C.E., meaning "before common era" and "common era," respectively. The change is simply one of semantics, language, a way of putting something across—that is, AD 100 is the same as 100 CE; all that changes is the label. The advocates of the switch from BC/AD to BCE/CE say that the newer designations are better in that they are devoid of religious connotation and thus prevent offending other cultures and religions who may not see Jesus as "Lord." What's religion got to do with it? It's history! It is ironic, of course, that something does distinguish a before and after. The thing that distinguishes B.C.E from C.E. is still the life and times of Jesus Christ. He isn't going away because He really is a character from history. He is the reason there is still a before and after.

4. RIGHT TIME
RIGHT PLACE

Long before time began to be recorded, God had determined the moment He would send Jesus into our world. That time would not come too early nor too late. Jesus came at the right time, the right moment, and in the right place. David recorded in a Psalm of how he had cried out, *"How long, O Lord?"* (Psalm 13:1). In his mind David thought the Lord had forgotten him because his enemies had got the upper hand. God had not and never would forget David. Having felt that way however, David never actually lost faith, because He knew deep inside that God had never let him down. God always had and always will save David, but He would do it when the time was right.

Prophets throughout the Old Testament asked the same question, "How long?". They were waiting for salvation, for His oppressed people to be rescued. God will provide what was needed when the time was right. Perhaps lessons had to be learnt first. Mary and Martha believed Jesus had missed that window of time needed to save their brother Lazarus who had died. Jesus had arrived three days too late, or so they thought (John 11:21). He wasn't late, He was on time for what he wanted to let them know. Men from the household of Jairus thought Jesus was too late to heal the synagogue ruler's daughter, they thought He should not now be troubled (Mark 5:35). Yet again Jesus' timing was perfect. In each situation, God confirmed that our timing is not His timing; He is always where He needs to be when He needs to be there.

At times, we may wonder about God's plan. We might stress over His apparent 'silence.' Our circumstances might lead us to believe all hope is lost. Yet God hasn't turned a blind eye or a deaf ear. He hasn't walked off leaving the job undone. His arms are not too short to reach us. Our prayers, our plans, our purpose for the future haven't gone up in a puff of smoke. God is still working in our lives even when we feel His not. Our limited understanding can't comprehend what God is thinking or planning. Based on what we see throughout the Bible we can be certain, if He 'delays' it's not because He's ignoring us but because He sees the bigger picture. It always turns out to be far greater than we could ever ask or imagine. His patience is often an act of mercy on those who still need to turn away from their sin and turn to Jesus.

Part of trusting God is to have faith in His timing. To trust God is to trust His way of doing things in His time. God loves us too much to answer prayers at any other time than the right time and in any other way than the right way. God works through human history His actions are not dictated to by what is happening at any given time. Jesus' arrival was not random chance. It was thought out, orderly and well prepared. He always existed but His arrival on earth came at the exact and precise time needed. This was to ensure we would understand and appreciate His message. If God could orchestrate all that was needed for our salvation through the events of history, we can surely trust Him with our own lives. When Paul wrote in Galatians about "the fullness of time" it refers to there being a plan that has been worked out. God did not wait until things looked or felt right. He knew the time; it had been predicted exactly when Jesus would come. There were many things occurring at the time of the first century that, at least by human reasoning, seem to make it ideal for Christ to arrive on the scene at that exact right time.

There was great anticipation among the Jews of that time that the Messiah would come. Coming from a history and background of false prophets, false messiahs, and misguided leadership to complete ignorance of the law and prophets, finally they were watching and waiting. The claustrophobic Roman rule kept Jews on the look-out for the promised Messiah to deliver them. Hadn't God delivered them from oppressors in the past? Surely, he will do the same again. There had been four hundred years of silence allowing God's people, in fact all people, to find out that they could not cope without God.

For the world to understand Jesus, it had to

understand why we need Jesus. That was the purpose of the Old Testament law. For generations God blessed and cursed, disciplined, cajoled, and pleaded with the Israelites to follow His will and accept His goodness. For generations, despite the fulfilled promises, giving of blessings and execution of punishment, they were unable to. If Jesus had come before the law was given and before the law failed, or rather the people failed to keep it, the need for and appreciation of His sacrifice would have been missed. A gift is most readily accepted when it's something we can't get for ourselves. They had to know as do we, you cannot do this, you cannot attain it yourself.

Paul pointed out in Galatians chapter four there was a period of being kept under a guardian, a tutor. The law was given to teach the difference between right and wrong. There was no doubt what is acceptable to God and what is not. The challenge was and is living by it. The teaching was good and accurate, but the students failed, they tried to wing it. They missed the point that it wasn't about going through the motions. The things they did were not merely fulfilling what was asked but had to be meaningful, heartfelt. Anything not done by faith was useless, pointless, a waste of time. What the people knew was, they couldn't be right without God, but he has been silent. It was time to ask once again, "How long?".

The time then came for the period of tutorship to end. It was time for people to be made free.

It is evident that God sought to lay a foundation through the Jewish Law that would prepare for the coming of the Messiah. The Law was meant to help people understand the depth of their sinfulness (in that they were incapable of keeping the Law) so that they might more readily accept the cure for that sin through Jesus the Messiah. Paul points out in Galatians chapter three verse twenty-three that those living under the law were being kept under guard in protective custody by it.

According to Romans chapter three the law took away any excuse for sinning because it taught what sin was. No one can keep it perfectly it only shows us what sin is. The Law was *"put in charge"*, Paul wrote in Galatians chapter three, to lead people to Jesus as the Messiah. The law pointed to Jesus. Its sacrificial system pointed to the need for a sacrifice for sin. The law was inadequate to save because no one could keep it perfectly. Add to this the many prophecies concerning the Messiah which were fulfilled in Jesus, and we realise the Old Testament is all about Him.

Throughout the Old Testament, God also showed how He interacts with historical events and eras. Egypt was a place the Israelites went to for refuge, God engineered the events that took them there. The life of Joseph a son of Jacob is a picture of the life of Christ. Through a series of what seemed like unfortunate events, God ensured Joseph was in Egypt before a great famine arose. He rose to be a kind of Prime Minister. Saving all of Egypt from the famine and then assisting nations around them, causing Egypt to become very powerful. Due to the good he had done Joseph's father, Jacob, and the whole family were welcomed into the country, resulting in the Israelites going through a kind of incubation period and growing into a large nation.

Years later a Pharoah who did not know all the good Joseph had done turned God's children into slaves. This caused them to cry out to God for help. God raised up Moses to shepherd the people. He rescued them and brought them into their own land with Joshua leading. God arranged things so that the natural animosity and belligerence of foreign nations corresponded to times that the Israelites needed to be judged. Provided He remained their God, they would be His people. But they didn't remain faithful to God, they wanted to do things their own way. God warned them, they ignored Him and so they were overtaken by neighbouring nations as they had been warned. After a while they cried out to God for rescue, and He then rescued them by raising up a judge. Eventually God had enough of this cycle of events, so the world power of the day invaded and took them over. There was a time God caused a Jewish girl by the name of Esther, to become queen to save her people from genocide. Living outside of time, God can see all of time and used events to have the desired effect on His plan, the spread of salvation to the world.

Old Testament history painted pictures of Christ through events such as the willingness of Abraham to offer up Isaac. Characters such as Joseph and religious feasts which can be seen in the details of the Passover during the exodus from Egypt all picture Jeus. Over and over, example after example, shadows of realities were given. Have you ever tried to explain something but the person you are talking to cannot quite grasp it? You ask, "Do I need to draw a picture for you?" Well, that is exactly what God did, in many ways. Even so some things were still not quite right in the people's theology. Somehow the picture they saw was not the one God had drawn.

A great number of Jews had the idea that freedom meant freedom on earth from worldly captors. That's what happened when they were slaves in Egypt then throughout their time in the Promised Land as judge after judge rescued them. Though this pointed to Jesus the salvation was not to be a release from any physical captivity but spiritual. People were deteriorating in their lusts as Paul pointed out in Romans chapter one. Yet the law didn't restrain them so what would? They had a law that said don't do this or you will be put to death, yet they still did it. Where is the deterrent if people just do not care about consequences but only fulfilling their selfish desires? Or maybe they thought God would not really punish them. The consequences were just a warning, God wouldn't really punish them, would He?

Are we any different? Times are hard and money is tight, but it is Christmas. What are you going to do? Perhaps it would be a good idea to cut back after all it is only one day of the year. One day followed by the consequence of months of debt until you have caught up. This is not a celebration authorised by God through the Bible and God certainly does not want us to be in debt. The Bible merely records the fact of Christ's birth. He came ultimately to pay our debt of sin. The debt for sin is the death of the sinner, which is separation from God. The law of Moses spelt out if you sin you die. Your sin can be covered over by the sacrifice of animals until Christ came. Jesus' death paid our debt, a debt we could not afford to pay, and He certainly did not owe, He was sinless. Our getting into debt and wondering how we will ever pay it off at least helps us understand our helplessness in overcoming the debt of sin. God knew we would do it so He put a plan into place, that He worked throughout the ages to save us because we cannot save ourselves. It would begin to come to fruition at the right time and in the right place.

5. HISTORY OF
THE WORLD

Long before time began to be recorded, God had determined the moment He would send Jesus into our world. That time would not come too early nor too late. Jesus came at the right time, the right moment, and in the right place. David recorded in a Psalm of how he had cried out, *"How long, O Lord?"* (Psalm 13:1). In his mind David thought the Lord had forgotten him because his enemies had got the upper hand. God had not and never would forget David. Having felt that way however, David never actually lost faith, because He knew deep inside that God had never let him down. God always had and always will save David, but He would do it when the time was right.

Prophets throughout the Old Testament asked the same question, "How long?". They were waiting for salvation, for His oppressed people to be rescued. God will provide what was needed when the time was right. Perhaps lessons had to be learnt first. Mary and Martha believed Jesus had missed that window of time needed to save their brother Lazarus who had died. Jesus had arrived three days too late, or so they thought (John 11:21). He wasn't late, He was on time for what he wanted to let them know. Men from the household of Jairus thought Jesus was too late to heal the synagogue ruler's daughter, they thought He should not now be troubled (Mark 5:35). Yet again Jesus' timing was perfect. In each situation, God confirmed that our timing is not His timing; He is always where He needs to be when He needs to be there.

At times, we may wonder about God's plan. We might stress over His apparent 'silence.' Our circumstances might lead us to believe all hope is lost. Yet God hasn't turned a blind eye or a deaf ear. He hasn't walked off leaving the job undone. His arms are not too short to reach us. Our prayers, our plans, our purpose for the future haven't gone up in a puff of smoke. God is still working in our lives even when we feel His not. Our limited understanding can't comprehend what God is thinking or planning. Based on what we see throughout the Bible we can be certain, if He 'delays' it's not because He's ignoring us but because He sees the bigger picture. It always turns out to be far greater than we could ever ask or imagine. His patience is often an act of mercy on those who still need to turn away from their sin and turn to Jesus.

Part of trusting God is to have faith in His timing. To trust God is to trust His way of doing things in His time. God loves us too much to answer prayers at any other time than the right time and in any other way than the right way. God works through human history His actions are not dictated to by what is happening at any given time. Jesus' arrival was not random chance. It was thought out, orderly and well prepared. He always existed but His arrival on earth came at the exact and precise time needed. This was to ensure we would understand and appreciate His message. If God could orchestrate all that was needed for our salvation through the events of history, we can surely trust Him with our own lives. When Paul wrote in Galatians about "the fullness of time" it refers to there being a plan that has been worked out. God did not wait until things looked or felt right. He knew the time; it had been predicted exactly when Jesus would come. There were many things occurring at the time of the first century that, at least by human reasoning, seem to make it ideal for Christ to arrive on the scene at that exact right time.

There was great anticipation among the Jews of that time that the Messiah would come. Coming from a history and background of false prophets, false messiahs, and misguided leadership to complete ignorance of the law and prophets, finally they were watching and waiting. The claustrophobic Roman rule kept Jews on the look-out for the promised Messiah to deliver them. Hadn't God delivered them from oppressors in the past? Surely, he will do the same again. There had been four hundred years of silence allowing God's people, in fact all people, to find out that they could not cope without God.

For the world to understand Jesus, it had to understand why we need Jesus. That was the purpose of the Old Testament law. For generations God blessed and cursed, disciplined, cajoled, and pleaded with the Israelites to follow His will and accept His goodness. For generations, despite the fulfilled promises, giving of blessings and execution of punishment, they were unable to. If Jesus had come before the law was given and before the law failed, or rather the people failed to keep it, the need for and appreciation of His sacrifice would have been missed. A gift is most readily accepted when it's something we can't get for ourselves. They had to know as do we, you cannot do this, you cannot attain it yourself.

Paul pointed out in Galatians chapter four there was a period of being kept under a guardian, a tutor. The law was given to teach the difference between right and wrong. There was no doubt what is acceptable to God and what is not. The challenge was and is living by it. The teaching was good and accurate, but the students failed, they tried to wing it. They missed the point that it wasn't about going through the motions. The things they did were not merely fulfilling what was asked but had to be meaningful, heartfelt. Anything not done by faith was useless, pointless, a waste of time. What the people knew was, they couldn't be right without God, but he has been silent. It was time to ask once again, "How long?".

The time then came for the period of tutorship

to end. It was time for people to be made free. It is evident that God sought to lay a foundation through the Jewish Law that would prepare for the coming of the Messiah. The Law was meant to help people understand the depth of their sinfulness (in that they were incapable of keeping the Law) so that they might more readily accept the cure for that sin through Jesus the Messiah. Paul points out in Galatians chapter three verse twenty-three that those living under the law were being kept under guard in protective custody by it.

According to Romans chapter three the law took away any excuse for sinning because it taught what sin was. No one can keep it perfectly it only shows us what sin is. The Law was *"put in charge",* Paul wrote in Galatians chapter three, to lead people to Jesus as the Messiah. The law pointed to Jesus. Its sacrificial system pointed to the need for a sacrifice for sin. The law was inadequate to save because no one could keep it perfectly. Add to this the many prophecies concerning the Messiah which were fulfilled in Jesus, and we realise the Old Testament is all about Him.

Throughout the Old Testament, God also showed how He interacts with historical events and eras. Egypt was a place the Israelites went to for refuge, God engineered the events that took them there. The life of Joseph a son of Jacob is a picture of the life of Christ. Through a series of what seemed like unfortunate events, God ensured Joseph was in Egypt before a great famine arose. He rose to be a kind of Prime Minister. Saving all of Egypt from the famine and then assisting nations around them, causing Egypt to become very powerful. Due to the good he had done Joseph's father, Jacob, and the whole family were welcomed into the country, resulting in the Israelites going through a kind of incubation period and growing into a large nation. Years later a Pharoah who did not know all the good Joseph had done turned God's children into slaves. This caused them to cry out to God for help. God raised up Moses to shepherd the people. He rescued them and brought them into their own land with Joshua leading.

God arranged things so that the natural animosity and belligerence of foreign nations corresponded to times that the Israelites needed to be judged. Provided He remained their God, they would be His people. But they didn't remain faithful to God, they wanted to do things their own way. God warned them, they ignored Him and so they were overtaken by neighbouring nations as they had been warned. After a while they cried out to God for rescue, and He then rescued them by raising up a judge. Eventually God had enough of this cycle of events, so the world power of the day invaded and took them over. There was a time God caused a Jewish girl by the name of Esther, to become queen to save her people from genocide. Living outside of time, God can see all of time and used events to have the desired effect on His plan, the spread of salvation to the world.

Old Testament history painted pictures of Christ through events such as the willingness of Abraham to offer up Isaac. Characters such as Joseph and religious feasts which can be seen in the details of the Passover during the exodus from Egypt all picture Jesus. Over and over, example after example, shadows of realities were given. Have you ever tried to explain something but the person you are talking to cannot quite grasp it? You ask, "Do I need to draw a picture for you?" Well, that is exactly what God did, in many ways. Even so some things were still not quite right in the people's theology. Somehow the picture they saw was not the one God had drawn.

A great number of Jews had the idea that freedom meant freedom on earth from worldly captors. That's what happened when they were slaves in Egypt then throughout their time in the Promised Land as judge after judge rescued them. Though this pointed to Jesus the salvation was not to be a release from any physical captivity but spiritual. People were deteriorating in their lusts as Paul pointed out in Romans chapter one. Yet the law didn't restrain them so what would? They had a law that said don't do this or you will be put to death, yet they still did it. Where is the deterrent if people just do not care about consequences but only fulfilling their selfish desires? Or maybe they thought God would not really punish them. The consequences were just a warning, God wouldn't really punish them, would He?

Are we any different? Times are hard and money is tight, but it is Christmas. What are you going to do? Perhaps it would be a good idea to cut back after all it is only one day of the year. One day followed by the consequence of months of debt until you have caught up. This is not a celebration authorised by God through the Bible and God certainly does not want us to be in debt. The Bible merely records the fact of Christ's birth. He came ultimately to pay our debt of sin. The debt for sin is the death of the sinner, which is separation from God. The law of Moses spelt out if you sin you die. Your sin can be covered over by the sacrifice of animals until Christ came. Jesus' death paid our debt, a debt we could not afford to pay, and He certainly did not owe, He was sinless. Our getting into debt and wondering how we will ever pay it off at least helps us understand our helplessness in overcoming the debt of sin. God knew we would do it so He put a plan into place, that He worked throughout the ages to save us because we cannot save ourselves. It would begin to come to fruition at the right time and in the right place.

6. REAL POWER
REAL SAVIOUR

The world before Caesar Augustus came along was in chaos. Rome's provinces were economically ruined. The generals and the higher class became wealthy at the expense of those under subjection to them. The rich became richer, the poor became poorer. People suffered from extortionate interest rates which gave rise to crooked money lending that led to ruined lives and a devastated economy. Money was lent out or was spent by the treasury without any real framework or plan. There were no checks or balances. We are told if you look after the pennies, the pounds will look after themselves. A failure to do this was disastrous on a large-scale Political corruption rose as it was easy to get away with and so it became rooted in the heart of Rome's government. When wealth did increase it only led to further political expenditure. Rome it was said by one commentator became a society of "intellectuals without morals" losing its previous moral and ethical qualities.

Rome was in a state of political turmoil and dysfunction before Caesar Augustus. The republic had existed for over 400 years but now it had finally hit a crisis that could not be overcome. Political guidelines or ethics that should have been standard were not being followed. If the government ran into a new problem, it would make amendments that would mean they could just carry on working and not worry about the collateral damage. Does that sound familiar?

During the first century before Christ, political violence, theft of land and death sentences became common[1]. To block the government and prevent anything getting done, senators would use what are known as bad faith arguments. That is, they would make an argument with the intention of deceiving or misleading the other party. It is not an authentic argument, and the one putting forward the argument wouldn't even believe it themselves. This type of argument obscures the core point of a debate rather than addressing the real issues. It is used to undermine an opponent's position by pushing them to defend an unrealistic or inaccurate version of their position. The opponent is misquoted so they must defend what they did not say because they have to state what they think about the content of the misquote. This derails them into an argument which has little to do with the original subject[2]. We too often hear it on modern day debates. It is how new bills run out of time to get put into law. There is nothing new under the sun.

At the time Augustus was born this was the kind of world people lived in. Most could not remember a time before all the land grabbing, killing of political enemies, procedural delays to legislation forming a status quo (not the group). There did not seem to be any good old days, everything was difficult and there seemed no end to it. Is it unique? Has it ever been any different? Perhaps only by lesser or greater degrees. It was a world wrecked by war, brutality, corruption, and immorality. Administration to benefit the citizens and protection for them had broken down; no one could feel safe. Robbers made every street unsafe at night; highwaymen roamed the roads, pirates sailed the seas kidnapping travellers, and selling them into slavery. Rome was full of men who had a purpose when out waging war but now these killing machines were home with nothing to do. How do you fill the vacuum? Their moral stability if they had any to begin with had disappeared. Soldiers who had tasted adventure on the battlefield knew how to kill and thought nothing of it. Citizens who had seen their savings consumed in the taxes and inflation of war waited in hope for a returning tide to lift them back to affluence and comfort; women given increasing freedom to do what they wanted when they wanted gained equality with men in their multiplying divorces, and adultery. That lifestyle choice led to unwanted pregnancies. Dealing with the disposal of the unwanted child risked the lives of most of the poorest women. It was only slightly less of a risk for the wealthy. And what of the unborn child? In that world, life was cheap!

They needed a Saviour. Someone to protect the poor from the rich. Rarely has it been different after all the idea and story of Robin Hood appears in many guises. A strong leader was needed to save the good politicians from losing their lives to the greedy less scrupulous politicians. Along came Augustus who replaced all this chaos with order. Augustus Caesar's birth name was Gaius Octavius. He was the nephew, adopted son, and hand-picked successor to Julius Caesar. Upon Julius' death, Octavian (as he was then called) had to fight to consolidate control. It wasn't pretty but the only way he could release Rome was to play them at their own game. He needed to defeat his rivals, but it couldn't be done through the ballot box. Those who had lived by the sword were going to find themselves dying by the sword. When he finally secured his position as the first Roman emperor, he reigned the longest of any of the Caesars in Julius' line, from 63 BC to AD 14. He received the name Augustus ("Venerable") in 27 BC. Augustus accepted Greek influences recognising they will be good for his people. He introduced Hellenistic literature alongside Roman literature and art. He expanded Rome's territory beyond what the eye can see. Augustus was more of a philosopher than a mere warfare leader. He learned from his great uncle Julius Caesar's mistakes and made Rome flourish greater and shine brighter than ever before both politically and economically.

Coincidentally, (not), Jesus was born in the reign

of Augustus. That is Augustus, the Saviour, the redeemer of the world. After a prolonged period of wars, political unity had been achieved. Augustus made himself Rome's first Emperor in 27BC. (Or if you prefer BCE. It makes little difference there was a defining line in history which was not about Augustus's birth). Building on the foundations laid by Julius Caesar, Augustus brought peace. This internal and international peace and order which Augustus achieved endured, with occasional interruptions, for about two centuries. Never had the known world been under one rule and never had they enjoyed such prosperity. As great a man as Caesar Augustus was, he was only a man. He of course demanded absolute power over the Roman Empire. Rome was not a republic, governed by laws made by various lawmakers now; it was an empire governed by an emperor.

The city of Rome ruled most of the Mediterranean world at that time. Within the empire there were citizens of Rome, who had special protections, and then everyone else. Conquered people did not have the same protection as citizens. Simply living within the borders of the Roman Empire did not automatically make you a citizen of Rome. Caesar Augustus is only mentioned once in the New Testament, at the beginning of the account recorded in Luke chapter two verse one: *"In those days Caesar Augustus issued a decree that a census should be taken of the entire Roman world"*. As a result of this decree, Joseph had to return to his ancestral home, Bethlehem, and he took with him Mary, who was already expecting the Baby Jesus. While they were there in Bethlehem, Jesus was born, as the prophet Micah had foretold: *"But you, Bethlehem Ephrathah, though you are small among the clans of Judah, out of you will come for me one who will be ruler over Israel, whose origins are from of old, from ancient times"* (Micah 5:2). The census that forced Joseph and Mary to go to Bethlehem was Augustus Caesar's most obvious impact on biblical history; however, there are other facts concerning Caesar Augustus that would have been meaningful to first-century readers of the Gospels.

Octavian was given the name Augustus, which means "great" or "venerable" or "worthy of reverence," which is an insinuation that he was worthy of worship. In 42 BC, the Senate formally deified Julius Caesar as "divus Iulius" ("the divine Julius"). This led to his adopted son, Octavian, being known as divi filius ("son of the god"), a title that Augustus Caesar embraced. Coins issued by Augustus featured Caesar's image and inscriptions such as "Divine Caesar and Son of God." An Egyptian inscription calls Augustus Caesar a star "shining with the brilliance of the Great Heavenly Saviour." In 17 BC an uncommon star did appear in the heavens; Augustus commanded a celebration, and Virgil pronounced, "The turning point of the ages has come."

During Augustus' reign, emperor worship exploded, especially in Asia Minor, which later became a hotbed for persecution of Christians. (Asia Minor was the area Paul covered in his first two missionary journeys as well as the location of the seven churches receiving letters in Revelation.) From what we know of Augustus and the worship that was paid to him, Luke is telling the story of Jesus in such a way that Christ is seen as the true possessor of the titles claimed by Augustus. It is not Augustus who is Savior and Lord, but *"Today in the town of David a Saviour has been born to you; he is Christ, the Lord"* (Luke 2:11). It is not Augustus, but Jesus who is the Son of God (Luke 1:32). And it is not in Augustus that the turning point of the ages has come, but in Jesus Christ, who ushers in the kingdom of God (Luke 4:43).

The Roman creed stated, "Caesar is Lord," but the Christian only recognizes Jesus as Lord. Because of their longstanding history of monotheism, Jews were granted an exemption from the required emperor worship. As long as Christianity was considered a sect of Judaism, Christians were also exempt from being forced to worship the Roman emperor. But as Jews began to denounce Christians and put them out of the synagogues, the Christians no longer were allowed this exception. Thus, the Roman government was the instrument of Jewish persecution in much of the New Testament. We see the first instance of this in the charges brought against Jesus Himself (Luke 23:1–2).

This happened again to Paul and Silas in Thessalonica, where some unbelieving Jews stirred up the crowd by saying, *"They are all defying Caesar's decrees, saying that there is another king, one called Jesus"* (Acts 17:7). Augustus Caesar died shortly after Jesus' birth. While Augustus himself may not have claimed the prerogatives of deity, he accepted divine titles as a means of propaganda. As the Roman religion developed, emperor worship became a patriotic duty. The New Testament refutes Roman religion at every turn, proclaiming Jesus, not Caesar, as the Son of God and Lord (Mark 1:1; 1 Thessalonians 1:1).

Augustus decreed the census. He brought about the human mechanism that God used to fulfil the prophecy regarding the place of the Messiah's birth. Augustus thought he was taking measure of the greatness of his kingdom, but he was setting the scene for his ultimate replacement. It was also under Augustus Caesar that the Roman peace was established, roads were built, and a common, stable culture was established so that the gospel could easily spread throughout the Roman Empire. While Augustus and the emperors after him thought they were building their own kingdom, they were simply unwitting and often unwilling actors in the building of the kingdom of God. This says something important about the world Jesus was born into. It was a world hungry for a Saviour, in a world that was living in the reign of a political saviour – Caesar Augustus – but he and what he accomplished was not enough. He was very useful though, in providing a way to the manger.

Along with knowing a lot from history about Augustus, we also know from history that Quirinius was governing Syria. The registration and census described was not for simple record-keeping or statistics. It was to efficiently and effectively tax everyone in the Roman Empire. The world responded to the command of Caesar Augustus. We are told in the Bible accounts, *"So all went to be registered".* One man, in the ivory palaces of Rome, gives a command – and the entire world responds!

It may well be that up to that point, there had never been a man with power over more lives than Caesar Augustus. However, Augustus was not powerful at all. In (John 19:10-11), Jesus confronted another Roman who believed he was powerful. *"Then Pilate said to Him, 'Are You not speaking to me? Do You not know that I have power to crucify You, and power to release You?'" Jesus answered, "You could have no power at all against Me unless it had been given you from above."* The same principle applies to Caesar Augustus.

Sitting in his palace making his decree, no doubt made him contemplate the power he had. Exercising his will in this way, the ultimate ruler making people move. But he was just a tool in God's hand. God had promised that the Messiah would be born in Bethlehem (Micah 5:2), and that promise would be fulfilled. How do you get a young couple from Nazareth down to Bethlehem when they had no reason or inclination to travel? Simple. Just work through the political "saviour of the world," and use him as a pawn in your plan. Let him provide a way to the manger for the real Saviour of the world. Augustus, for all his accomplishments, could not really be the answer to the world's problems. God allowed Caesar Augustus to rise to unheard of human power for his purpose not Rome's. He was, it could be said, a "Roman John the Baptist" preparing the way for Jesus. At the end of it all Jesus is the main character. Who does the world know more about today – Jesus or Caesar Augustus? Who has the legacy?

The trip from Nazareth to Bethlehem is about eighty miles. This was not a short distance in those days. It was a significant undertaking, costing time and money. We often think that Mary was close to delivery when they made this journey, but this may not have been the case at all. According to Roman law, Mary did not have to go with Joseph for the tax census; but it made sense for her to go with him, especially because she was in the latter stages of a controversial pregnancy we are not told as much but she could have been the subject of gossip in Nazareth. It is possible that Joseph used the emperor's order as a means of removing Mary from gossip and emotional stress in her own village. Luke tells us that it was while they were in Bethlehem, *"And while they were there, the time came for her baby to be born"* One of the striking things about Luke's account is how simple it contrasts with how great the events are. Our modern world hypes meaningless events so much like TV talent shows, or competitions amongst celebrities we have not heard of. It is hard for us to appreciate how simply stated this greatest of events is.

Augustus the ruler of the known world without knowing it made sure the Saviour of the entire world would be laid in a manger in Bethlehem fulfilling prophecy. God became flesh into a world made ready for Him by political events. Events that would lead to His death on the cross to save sinful humanity. The real Saviour, with the real power.

FOOTNOTES 1 history.com

7. SHEPHERD'S VISIT THE SHEPHERD'S SHEPHERD

After the great Emperor Caesar Augustus made sure that the Saviour of the world would be born in Bethlehem, how would the pronouncement be made? Surely if God used such a mighty and powerful man to fulfil his purpose the announcement would be made by someone just as important. Today there would be a proclamation at the Palace, Parliament would be reconvened, the Prime Minister would have to cut short his holiday, all the news channels and papers would be full of the news, the internet would crash with a rush to announce and read of such an event. Social media would be abuzz with people rushing to get there and take a selfie to prove it. Well... in Luke chapter two and verse eight we are told shepherds are watching over their flocks, I know a song about that! Then in verse nine we read that an angel made an announcement, I know a song about that too!

Interrupting what would be a night like any other night for this group of shepherds was the unmissable brightness of the presence of an angel and "the glory of the Lord". The angel brought "good tidings" to these shepherds, who in the society of their day were regarded as social outcasts. As a class of people in that day shepherds had a bad reputation. More regrettable was their habit of confusing 'mine' with 'thine' as they moved about the country. They were considered unreliable to the extent they were not even allowed to give testimony in the law courts. It is to these people the announcement was made; *"For there is born to you this day in the city of David a Saviour".* Why were they chosen? The birth of a Saviour demands a grand announcement in keeping with his stature. Was the task given to a President, Prime Minister, or a committee such as the United Nations? It was not given first to royalty, governors, or rulers but to lowly shepherds.

A Saviour, which is what the world really needs, should surely be announced to someone much further up the social scale. Someone who would be listened to because of their status. Suddenly there was with the angel a multitude of the heavenly host praising God. After the single angel's announcement, a whole group of angels appeared. That's more like it! This was a heavenly host that proclaimed peace. Something the world needed then and needs now. The one who can bring peace to the world has just been born. The job of announcing he was now here was given to... shepherds? The shepherds didn't hesitate when they were told "come and see the child Jesus". The words *"Let us go now",* shows urgency. They didn't question or wait. The angel told them to look for a baby lying in a manger. We read of it in Luke chapter two and verse twelve. It wasn't an unusual sight to see a baby wrapped in clothes, but it was perhaps strange to see a baby lying in a feeding trough. If the angel had not told them to look for this specific sign, where would they have looked? Where would they expect such a child to be? Where would you expect to see the new-born Saviour of the world? The king?

The shepherds found Mary and Joseph in very humble surroundings. A place they themselves had no worries about approaching. Had he been in a palace the shepherds would have thought twice about starting the journey let alone entering the grounds. This was a place that was accessible to them. They saw the baby in a manger just as the angel had said. What a strange sight! What could be more improbable than to believe that he was the King when born into these humble circumstances. Who would have thought they would be the first to see him?

Having seen what they had, or rather who they had, Luke tells us the shepherds went on to spread the news of Jesus' birth. It no longer mattered to them how they would be received they had a message that needed to be shared. What conversation did they have with Joseph and Mary? What did Joseph and Mary think when these strangers turned up and asked if they could see the baby? They had been visited by an angel who gave them this new. Both Joseph and Mary could relate to that, it would give credence to why they were there.

We also read that *"Mary kept all these things and pondered them in her heart"*. Mary had good reason to meditate. The visit from the angel. Feeling pregnant with all that goes with it. How did she and Joseph end up in Bethlehem? The emperor's great decree from Rome reached down to them. Were there gossiping tongues in Nazareth? God works through all kinds of people and all kinds of events to accomplish His plan. From emperors to shepherds.

This is so incredible once we take time to consider all these events together. Not as a children's story, but a factual account. Not a Christmas song or poem, but events based in history at an actual time and in a real place. Just think who God used to fulfil His purpose. From the most powerful, to the most powerless. Some were totally oblivious, others willingly following what they were asked to do. How much more can he use us now to proclaim His good news knowing all that we now know.

It does not matter who you are, or who you think you are, the story of Jesus birth lets us know God's purpose will be fulfilled. Whether a King or a shepherd God is no respecter of persons, he used them then, he can use you now. The way in a manger was the way the truth and life for all people. Everyone lives on the earth God created. Some acknowledge that fact others do not. The question is will you be a willing or unwilling participant in the Way the Truth and the Life?

8. THREE GIFTS.

One year in the nativity at infant school I played the part of the shepherd who brought a lamb for the baby Jesus. The one thing I had to remember was the lamb. So of course, I remembered that once we arrived at the manger. I tried to quietly dash off stage in front of everyone to go and fetch it from the classroom/changing room. As far as I can remember no one noticed. The next year I was the servant of the king/wise man who took gold to Jesus. This time I remembered and managed to keep the gold on the cushion as we walked up the centre aisle of the school hall. Quite a task as I also wanted to wave to my mum and grandma whilst balancing the cushion with one hand.

The script called for three kings or wise men. To give more children the opportunity to star in the show instead of having more kings, the kings each had a servant. If you check the original account there is not a number given, we could have had as many as we wanted in our play. Were they even kings? What do we know or assume about these people who figure so prominently in Nativity plays and are sung about without fail each year? We read about them in Matthew chapter two, the first book of the New Testament. They were astrologers, stargazers. And they had no doubt what the new star they had found meant. It could only be the birth of the promised king in Judah. They were probably gentiles not Jewish as seen in them referring to him as the king of the Jews, not "our King". Tradition, not the Gospels, says the Magi, another word for them, were three kings. Having three gifts has led to the thought that there were three. And there is no evidence at all that they were kings, maybe it's just that the term "wise men" does not rhyme in the carol. Time had obviously passed since Jesus had been born and laid in a manger, we are told they came to the "house" in Matthew chapter two verse eleven. Enough time had passed for him to no longer be a baby. The cave where the animals were stabled was only a temporary shelter. The wise men saw the "child" with his mother, not a baby.

The news of a new king was not welcome at the palace. Herod was king of the Jews though only by permission of the Romans, and the astrologers were supposed to let him know where the new king was so he could "pay his respects". However, the truth was he did not want any rivals. In his position he was on to a good thing. The dreadful massacre of the infants is in keeping with other cruelties mentioned in historical records of that evil man. The picture that the word massacre suggests is of many, many people suffering. There would not be many boys of that age in the area so fewer than the number we would usually think of were involved. Having said that it is still an horrendous thing for him to order, for soldiers to carry out and parents and siblings to be scarred for life over. The family of Jesus escaped to Egypt, just as his ancestor Jacob and his family had done as recorded in Genesis, long before when famine struck. Which itself is a picture of what would happen to the Saviour when he would be born.

The presents given to the baby had special significance - gold for a king; incense for a priest; myrrh for a mortal man. All picture something about Jesus. When the Israelites entered the land of Canaan, gold and silver formed part of the spoils of war. Jewellers probably made ornaments and jewellery for those who could afford them. In times of religious decline, they adopted the practices of the surrounding nations and made idols of silver or gold. (This custom was strongly criticized by the prophets.) The process of refining gold and silver - melting it to separate off the impurities - is often used in the Bible as a picture of the purifying effects of suffering.

By offering gold as a gift these men recognised the kingship of Jesus. But there is also a foretelling of the suffering which must be endured to produce purity. Jesus had to suffer so that we could be presented as pure before our Father.

Gum is collected by peeling back the bark of the frankincense-tree and cutting into the trunk. The resin gives off a sweet scent when warmed or burned and was used as incense in Bible times. In Exodus chapter thirty verses one to ten the altar of incense is described in the Holy Place as being next to the veil. When it was lit as the incense burned, so the fragrance wafted into the Most Holy Place. The only access to the Holy Place was through the entrance from the courtyard, and the airflow therefore was one way, it went from the priests and people and into the Most Holy Place where God was. The incense was to burn continuously and in the same way we are to offer up our own sacrifice of prayer to the Lord as it is called in Hebrews chapter thirteen and verse fifteen.

In the early church we can see the importance of prayer as the disciples devoted themselves to it along with fellowship, the breaking of bread and the teaching of the apostles. Jesus is described as our intercessor. Here again we see an indication of what Jesus was here for. He gained access to God for us so we can enter his presence and pray with confidence. Incense used by the priests is symbolic of that.

Myrrh is a pale-reddish gum from a shrub which grows in Somalia, Ethiopia, and Arabia. For many years it has been used as a spice and a medicine. It was also used in making the holy oil for the tabernacle and temple. It was mixed with the drink offered to Jesus on the cross as a painkiller in Mark chapter fifteen verse twenty-three, but Jesus did not take it. Joseph and Nicodemus later embalmed Jesus' body with myrrh and aloes. It was very expensive and usually used in Royal burials. To receive this gift at birth indicated he was born to die. You might say we all are, but his death was on our behalf, for our benefit.

The gold was for a King. Frankincense was for a priest; myrrh was for someone at death. While Jesus was still a child these men foretold that He was the true King, the perfect High Priest, and the Saviour of all who will give their lives to him by accepting his gift to us.

It was one thing for Mary to be told she was pregnant with the Promised Messiah, and Joseph to be told he would share in raising him. They would surely have known that the Messiah would be put to death at some point for the forgiveness of the world's sin. Or did they? Did they fully comprehend all that this would mean. Put yourself in their place as the Shepherds visited at the birth. Then as they had escaped to Egypt and then had these, what looked like, important people arrive. As the gifts were offered, did they say, "Oh no you shouldn't, that's far too much. We hardly know you."? They now have a baby to hold and be in the presence of, the dream was now a reality. Have you been in that privileged position of returning home from the hospital with the baby? Getting in the house, setting down the car seat looking at your bundle of joy and thinking, "Now what do we do?" This is it, there is no time off ever again, it's all about the baby. As these meaningful gifts were being given did Mary and Joseph realise straight away what they meant? If the events surrounding the birth of Christ mean anything at all, it has to do with the eventual death and resurrection of Jesus. Was that fully understood by them?

Jesus did not save us from our sins by his birth but by his death. His birth was necessary for Him to be fully human. Without being human His sacrifice would not pay our debt. Perhaps it is significant that his birth is remembered once a year and his resurrection is remembered every week. His birth is pointless if His life did not end with our salvation. The "Wise" men understood the relevance of his birth. These gifts spoke of who Jesus was and what he was here for. May we come to know Jesus as our King, Priest, and Saviour. That would be the wise thing to do!

9. WHAT ARE YOU WAITING FOR?

No other month, except the one you have your birthday in, has the days ticked off and counted down as December does. My mum and mother-in-law have their birthdays in mid-December so there are two countdowns. My wife has her birthday in December but after Christmas. She would claim only one countdown counts.

Around October in various ways and on various social media platforms we begin to be told how many shopping days there are until Christmas. People say, "We haven't even had bonfire night yet", however, no one counts down to that. Once we get to November and the fireworks have hardly quietened down, Christmas songs become more prevalent in shops and on the radio. Then on December 1st the advent calendars are allowed to be put up and the serious countdown begins. As children in our family, we had one that came out every year. The door of the day was opened and revealed a Christmas or Nativity themed picture. That was it. My children began with one that had chocolate behind each door. On their day on opening the window they were the one who had the chocolate.

One year as windows were opened the chocolate had already disappeared. This led to them having a calendar each so there were no arguments. For the past few years Suzanne introduced the idea of having a Bible verse to read on each day too. For some, chocolate just is not enough. Recently I heard of a specialist cheese one. I googled and found one on the market with jewellery behind each door which once it was all opened was valued at £104,000.

Why do we count down the days of December? Why has doing so become so extravagant. The answer, I think, is that December has with it an anticipation. Something to look forward to in the bleak mid-winter. Is the countdown worth it? What are you waiting for this Christmas? What are you waiting for anyway? Are you longing for anything? Are you looking forward to something, anything that might give your life hope or purpose? Something to pick you up, lift your spirit, something to make your life worthwhile.

In the Gospel of Luke, we come across two characters who make their appearance in the final scene of the events surrounding Christ's birth. One is a man named Simeon; the other is a woman named Anna. They don't appear in any nativity scenes or on Christmas cards, but they are significant in the Biblical account. Both individuals were waiting for something or should I say, they were waiting for someone. Things weren't going well for the nation of Israel. No word had been heard from God for around four hundred years. Having overthrown and thrown out their Greek oppressors they had now come under Roman rule. They had lost their political independence and couldn't make any of the important decisions for themselves. They were living in fear of the crafty, and very cruel King Herod. Many were wondering if the Saviour would ever come and deliver them from their enemy. God had never failed them in the past, even though they repeatedly failed Him. Had He finally had enough? Were they being left to their own devices?

Simeon had good reason for the hope within him and anticipation that brought because: *"…he would not die before he had seen the Lord's Christ."* The Holy Spirit prompted Simeon to go to the temple courts at just the right time on just the right day that Joseph and Mary were bringing their infant to the Temple. When Simeon looked at the baby Jesus, he knew straightaway that God's promise had been kept.

The other Character waiting with anticipation was Anna. The Bible says that she never left the temple but worshipped day and night. She was looking forward to the same person as Simeon, but instead of looking for comfort, Anna was looking for forgiveness. Verse thirty-eight of Luke chapter two tells us, *"Coming up to them at that very moment, she gave thanks to God and spoke about the child to all who were looking forward to the redemption of Israel."*

When Jesus came, He provided the very things that Simeon and Anna were waiting for. That is, someone who will save the people from their sin, which would bring God's comfort and His forgiveness.

Whilst Christmas and what it has become might be a bit of light in the dark winter months, or warmth in the cold, the reality behind the fantasies offers so much more. Life-changingly more. You can experience God's comfort and forgiveness, not by celebrating Christmas but following Jesus.

Christmas loses its edge the older and more familiar with it you get. Let's face it, Christmas was always better in the past. We don't even have Morecambe and Wise Christmas Specials on the telly now. Its predictable, too commercial, and more for kids. Unless you like a drink, then it provides so many excuses to imbibe more than you usually can get away with. Then there is the food! Maybe it is for more than the kid after all. You hear the story so much that it no longer astonishes you? Lofty religious thoughts about it not being the date and not commanded and we shouldn't really do it and maybe the tree is pagan, all distracts from an actual historical event that has meaning for the whole world.

I'm not advocating keeping Christ in Christmas. I'm saying don't let all that now surrounds it distract you from marvelling and being amazed at what God has done through his Son. Something that happened in history.

The miracle of the virgin birth, the fulfilment of all the Old Testament prophecies, God becoming flesh, let us not deny the truth or play down the actual event. History was split in two at the birth of Jesus. There was the world before He was born and the world after. History references a before Christ and after he came to earth. A historical event we cannot ignore. Be amazed at what God has done in sending His son at the right time to the right place in the right way, to set anyone free from sin who will respond to him.

Mary responded when she said to the angel, *"May it be to me as you have said."* Joseph woke up from his dream and *"...did what the angel of the Lord had commanded and took Mary home as his wife."* The Shepherds said, *"Let's go to Bethlehem and see this thing that has happened..."* The wise men saw the star and moved out of the safety of their home, risking their lives to find the new king.

It is a time of year to be enjoyed but it is meaningless if you pack Jesus away with the decorations when it is over. Better to move closer to Christ through the message of the good news about him. Summer Holidays and sales start to be advertised on Boxing Day to give you something else to look forward to. For many, Christmas isn't merry, and the New Year isn't happy, and it won't be until we surrender our lives to Christ. The grown up one that is. What's the point of all this Christmas stuff unless you move from it to the grown-up Jesus.

The Bible story begins in the beginning with Genesis and concludes in the last book of the Bible, Revelation. Just a few verses are given over to the birth of Christ. All that was written before looked forward to that event. That event led to the central point which is that Jesus Christ was crucified, dying to gain you forgiveness from your sin, and raising up from the grave to show that you too can live forever with Him.

The wonder of Christ's birth and how it fits in to the biblical story is astonishing. What is more astonishing is the hope the life that Jesus gave on your behalf can bring. You look forward to Christmas but what then? Apply that question to your life. You leave school but what then? You get a job and then retire, but what then? You retire, but what then? The whole reason for the season answers the "What then?" of your life. Everything that happened was and is for you and your salvation. Ultimately Jesus gave his life for you. What then? What are you waiting for?

10. NAME THE BABY.

A quick search on the internet has just informed me that the most popular boys name in recent years is Noah. Prior to that it was Liam and before that Oliver. For the girls it is Olivia. Amelia and Isla follow closely behind. It is interesting to go back over the years and see what names were popular at different times and in different decades. Trends often follow what is going on in society at the time with royal births, film, television, and celebrities.

Names in the Bible are regarded as important, knowing why they were chosen tells us something about the child or their birth (Isaac means "laughter", Benjamin means "son of the right hand", Esau means "hairy"). Some names were changed to signal a drastic change in life (Abram to Abraham, Sarai to Sarah, Jacob to Israel, Saul to Paul).

A name is important because it's not just a word, it's who you are. Solomon wrote: *"A good name is to be chosen rather than great riches."* (Prov. 22:1) There is no name more significant than "Immanuel". This name, which Matthew refers to in his Gospel (Matthew 1:23), was first given to Jesus by the prophet Isaiah 700 years before His birth (Isaiah 7:14). And this very special name, as Matthew tells us, means "God with us." Jesus Christ is Immanuel,

"God with us." The baby born to Mary in a manger, the infant that the shepherds ran to see, the new-born child that the Magi travelled hundreds of miles to worship is Immanuel, God with us. But in what sense is Jesus "God with us?"

Wasn't God our creator always with his creation, his people? Yes. In one sense God, the Creator, has always been "with" His creation. Unlike the false gods of paganism or theistic evolutionists, who believe in a god who started the world and then left it to run itself. The one true God who created us has always been with us. This is spoken of by God through Jeremiah (23:23-24); *"Am I a God who is only close at hand?" says the LORD. "No, I am far away at the same time. Can anyone hide from me in a secret place? Am I not everywhere in all the heavens and earth?" says the LORD."* The God of the Bible, our Creator is everywhere at the same time. All of creation is filled with His presence; from mountains to molecules; and yet He is not a part of that creation. He is Creator distinct from His creation.

We read of Paul in Acts 14, preaching to the people of Lystra, who being pagans, worshipped many different gods. He reminded them that God, the Creator, had always been with them, giving them witness or proof of Himself by providing them with rain, sunshine fruitful seasons, and giving them food. God has always been with His creation in the sense that He, who is everywhere, has showered all people with blessings despite their sin. He sends his sunshine and rain on the righteous and unrighteous. He is no respecter of persons, all benefit from His goodness and mercy.

With the birth of Jesus Christ in Bethlehem, Immanuel, "God with Us," takes on a special meaning. In the man Jesus, God is "with us" because Jesus is God. What sent the shepherds back to the fields rejoicing? What made the wise men worship in wonder? It was the realization that they were in the presence of their Creator made human. Years later John under the inspiration of the Spirit would write the perfect commentary on these events. *"In the beginning was the Word, and the Word was with God, and the Word was God. He was in the beginning with God; and all things were made through Him and apart from Him nothing was made which was made...And the Word became flesh and dwelt among us, and we beheld His glory, glory as of the only begotten of the Father, full of grace and truth"* (John 1:1-3, 14).

The true message of Christ coming to live on earth staggers the imagination: The only begotten Son of the Father, the eternal Word, our Creator, clothed Himself in our physical nature, and became human, one of us. God Himself lay in the manger, completely human, completely Divine. Completely helpless and in need of the care of His parents. The message of the gospel began at creation and continued from the birth of Jesus to his death and resurrection. All that time God is with us.

Peter spoke to the thousands gathered on the

day of Pentecost in Acts chapter two about Jesus Christ. He did not just point out the fact that Jesus had been crucified and buried, but that he was also raised from the dead to sit at the right hand of God. The crowd of people was convicted of the role they had played in the rejection of Jesus. They wanted to do something about this terrible mistake they now knew they had made. They were told by Peter, *"Each of you must repent of your sins and turn to God and be baptized in the name of Jesus Christ for the forgiveness of your sins. Then you will receive the gift of the Holy Spirit. This promise is to you, to your children, and to those far away — all who have been called by the Lord our God."* (Acts 2:38-39). One of the many great things about Jesus Christ is that his blessings are available to everyone, to you, your family, your neighbours and even those who are "far off." The people of Peter's day and their descendants. Everyone.

The birth of Christ is part of the gospel story but for many their association with Christ begins on Christmas Eve and ends on Boxing Day. The original intent of keeping the Sabbath day was for parents to teach their children about God's creation. He created over six days and rested on the seventh. The importance of rest is emphasised. It later took on extra significance once they were freed from slavery. In Egypt they were slaves and had no rest. Once in their own land they were commanded to rest, to have a day off, but not without purpose. They were to tell the generations that came along and were distanced by time to the difficult time in Egypt; "We've got a day off, we never used to when we were slaves but listen while I tell you what God has done for us."

Is this time of year a humbug? Getting in the way of real life. For many it is a depressing time watching others over-indulge whilst you or your loved one's struggle to make ends meet. For some it intensifies loneliness, heightens the feelings of loss. If this time of year is stressful and leads to those thoughts, stop concentrating on the birth of Christ and consider who He claims to be because of that birth. The few verses in the Bible that tell us about His birth, are there to confirm the prophecies spoken of Him. The point is God came to be with us, that is something to be glad about. God is with us, that has deeper meaning, when you can you truly say you are with Him.

11. HAPPY BIRTHDAY.

What a pity for Jesus, being born on Christmas day. At least that's how we view things now for those who might only get one present to cover both days at once. Being born too near Christmas day can overshadow your big day. No one really knows the day of Jesus' birth it was not necessary to record it. The Bible gives no hint of the year or time of year. In fact, the numbering of year one was not done until many years later. If there was to be a great remembrance of it more details of when and how would have been recorded. The early Christian writer Origen of Alexandria (165 – 264) mocks the Roman practice of celebrating birthdays as "pagan". With this in view the early Christians would not mark the birthday of Jesus as they wouldn't even celebrate their own with it being a pagan practice.

The first recorded date of Christmas being celebrated on December 25th was in 336AD, during the time of the Roman Emperor Constantine. There are many theories as to why this date was chosen. One is because the Winter Solstice and the ancient pagan Roman midwinter festivals called 'Saturnalia' and 'Dies Natalis Solis Invicti' took place. It was when winter ended and spring began, a festival was held to welcome the return of the sun god. As a celebration was taking place at that time of year anyway the date was taken over. By taking over the holiday it was thought Christianity and knowledge of the one true God could be spread. Another theory is that the date corresponds to Hanukkah when the Jews celebrated being able to worship in the temple again. Also known as the festival of lights, candles were lit on successive days. Jesus is the light of the world, so this was a good time to celebrate the birth of Jesus. Hanukkah or the Feast of Dedication was not authorised by scripture. But it was a vital reminder of a great rescue. It's interesting to note that Jesus never spoke against the celebration though He was present as it was going on.

The association with paganism distracts us and causes many Christians to shy away from spending a great deal of time acknowledging the birth of Christ. Many will enjoy the holiday but, in an attempt, not to get close to pagan practices they practically ignore the birth of Jesus. The facts against knowing the date of Jesus birth are plain to see. We do not know when Christ was born. Neither are we told to have any kind of celebration of his birth, but he was born! The birth of Jesus fulfilled numerous Old Testament prophecies given centuries before the events they described. Matthew in his gospel, (1:22), introduces a common statement, *"So all this was done that it might be fulfilled which was spoken by the Lord through the prophet."* Using this phrasing in at least a dozen passages, Matthew knew it was important to point out to his readers that many of the events he described fulfilled specific prophecies.

The first prophecy being spoken of as "fulfilled" introduces one of the best-known clues to the Saviour in the Bible. *"Behold, the virgin shall be with child, and bear a Son, and they shall call His name Immanuel,"* which is translated, *"God with us."* In reference to the birth of Jesus, Matthew reminds the readers of this specific prophecy from Isaiah made more than seven hundred years earlier. *"Therefore, the Lord Himself will give you a sign: Behold, the virgin shall conceive and bear a Son, and shall call His name Immanuel".* Mary did conceive and gave birth to a son who is called Immanuel though she was a virgin. This amazing event demonstrates God's infinite knowledge and power. He foretold the future with perfect precision, and He has the power to bring His prophecies to fulfilment even if that meant a virgin would need to conceive and bear a Son.

After Christ's birth the magi or wise men, or kings, arrived in Jerusalem. Herod gathered them the chief priests and scribes and asked them all where the Messiah was going to be born. They responded by citing an Old Testament prophecy pinpointing Bethlehem as the birthplace of the Christ: *"But you, Bethlehem, in the land of Judah, are not the least among the rulers of Judah; For out of you shall come a Ruler who will shepherd My people, Israel."* (Compare Matthew 2:6, Micah 2:5 and John 7:42).

Herod's murderous response of slaughtering the young boys of Bethlehem led to the fulfilment of three more prophecies. First, this tragic massacre fulfilled the words of Jeremiah. *"A voice was heard in Ramah, lamentation, weeping, and great mourning, Rachel weeping for her children, refusing to be comforted, because they are no more."* (Compare Matthew 2:18 with Jeremiah 31:15).

The original context of this prophecy had to do with mothers in Israel lamenting the deportation of their sons to Babylon. They were personified as 'Rachel,' the beloved wife of Jacob, whose sons Joseph and Benjamin had also been threatened with being 'no more' (i.e., carried away into Egypt; see Genesis 42:36). Ramah was a town close to Jerusalem and associated with Rachel's tomb (1 Samuel 10:2-3). The second fulfilled prophecy resulting from Herod's paranoiac rage took place after Joseph took Mary and Jesus to Egypt. On their return, God's words to Hosea were fulfilled. *"Out of Egypt I called My Son."* (Matthew 2:15 see also Hosea 11:1). This prophecy was originally made as a statement of history. God had called (and brought) Israel out of Egypt. Guided by the Holy Spirit, Matthew used these words to refer to the Messiah. Many other prophecies could be listed that were perfectly fulfilled in the life of Jesus Christ. These were not lucky guesses made by frauds; they were precise predictions made by the all-knowing God of the Bible. Consequently, we can be completely confident that He will always fulfil His promises.

Just over 2,000 years ago, Jesus came to earth in humble circumstances. The Saviour of the world and God of all creation became human, put on humanity, to die for our sins and gain our victory over death by conquering it Himself. This gives the hope of salvation to all who turn from their sin and believe on Him. This is not dependant on knowing the date of His birth. It is not dependant on remembering or celebrating His birthday. That is neither here nor there. The fact is Jesus Christ was born in Bethlehem in fulfilment of prophecy. One day, He will return in judgment, and He will not appear as a seemingly helpless baby, but as the risen, glorified, sovereign Lord and Judge. He has foretold it; and because of the many previously fulfilled prophecies concerning Him we can believe it.

12. BAD NEWS ABOUT CHRISTMAS

For many people Christmas is not merry, and the New Year is not happy, there is nothing be merry about or celebrate. There are some extremely difficult circumstances that people live with. These are things that do not dissipate just because it is Christmas. In its extreme there are those whose circumstances have resulted in them being homeless and living on the street, far from what was their home. Difficulty with addictions, relationships that have broken down, ostracised from family maybe through no fault of their own. Each day is a struggle just to survive. There are illnesses and terminal disease that do not suddenly go away for a few days. It is a time of year that heightens the sense of loss amongst people who still mourn loved ones. Christmas is full of too many once happy but now painful memories. You can cope usually but there is something about that time of year that triggers thoughts of what might have been or now should be.

The need to "push the boat out", causes debt which can last well into the following year. You don't want your children to miss out. It's only once a year. We talk ourselves into ensuring a good time is had by our family resigning ourselves to a lot of overtime the following month or two. The stress of shopping for presents and food and all the preparation that goes along with it can almost push some to a nervous breakdown. The pressure is not just financial. Sadly, couples and families fall out and even get torn apart and all for what? Decorations, trees, food, presents, booze, and parties, none of those things have anything to do with the biblical account of Christ's birth. Traditions that have built up around the holiday are what have pushed us to the limit. Today Christmas for many is actually bad news.

Would it surprise you to know that for all the joy announced at the birth of Jesus and that we are now supposed to enjoy at this time of year, the birth of Jesus was bad news. The whole reason God joined us on earth, was not to institute an overblown birthday party. He came to deal with a problem that had existed since creation When Adam and Eve first sinned and punishment was pronounced, God straightaway made a promise and prophesied that He would rescue us from the punishment of our sin.

What we sing about in the Christmas carols, and we read about in Matthew and Luke's gospel accounts of his birth are simple yet profound. It is utterly amazing that God our creator could join us on earth as a human. God made flesh. The creator of the world laying in a manger in what at the time was a little-known town. God subjected himself to what we all face in this terribly broken and dysfunctional world. Brought up by Joseph and Mary, experiencing all that is common to us hunger, thirst, temptation, joy, sorrow, heat, cold, injustice, pain and ultimately death.

As hard as it is to is to understand how he was fully God and fully man, it is just as hard to understand why he would put himself through all of that, especially for us. God came to earth, apparently to save us. To be saved from something harmful is a relief. Could there ever be better news than this? However, knowing what God did through Jesus and how that was accomplished tells us why the Christmas story is in reality bad news.

God did what he did because there was no other way, he could help us. In the pages of the Bible, we are described as His "special possession". The Jews of His day were expecting the kind of Saviour who had always come along and saved them from their physical enemy. They were due for a Saviour to appear now and kick out the Romans who they were in subjection to.

The problem is that this was not their biggest problem. Neither is it ours. If the only thing human beings needed was a little help with their behaviour or a tweaking of their life circumstances, then the coming of Jesus to earth wouldn't make any sense. But if the greatest danger to all of us is within us, then Jesus is our only hope. People can leave difficult relationships, resign, and walk away from a bad career or job. Those who want a change can move from a dangerous part of town, even walk away from church that isn't as it ought to be. But how do you escape from yourself. My biggest problem is me. Wherever I go there I am. Without the birth of Jesus and all that followed I'd be lost. The bad news of Christmas is that it confirms the problem we have which is stated in Romans chapter three and verse twenty-three, *"all have sinned and fall short of the glory of God."* Sin is the bad news of the Christmas story. Jesus didn't come to earth to give us a day off with presents and good food. That doesn't solve anything and the pressure of it can in many cases make things worse. Jesus came on a mission to rescue us not just give us a few days off to have a good time and forget our problems.

Sin separates us from God and makes us guilty before him. Sin makes us active enemies against God, we are not passive bystanders. Sin blinds us to the serious condition we are in and our utter need for help. Sin causes us to replace worshiping God with entertainment that pleases us. We use created things to try and satisfy ourselves. Sin makes us unable to live as we were designed to live. Sin is a disease, a plague, that we cannot overcome ourselves. What makes the Christmas story bad news is that it tells us something more than the story itself. That is, Jesus knew that even if we were aware of the great danger of sin, we could not help ourselves. Sin is the ultimate undefeatable enemy.

We convince ourselves we are in control until we realise, we are captive to it. It is either the height of arrogance or the depth of delusion to think that you are okay. The only possible thing that can make us right with God is that Christ came to earth as a baby. God made a way to the manger, but Jesus made His way out of it and grew to be the man that saved us.

There is a way we try to rid ourselves of this bad news. When you do something wrong, you blame it on everything but yourself. Stress or sickness, a bad boss, a spouse that doesn't understand, a rebellious child, or some other pressure of life. But if someone points out where you are in the wrong, is your response to thank them? To be thankful someone cared enough to tell you. Or do you jump to your own defence, how dare they suggest you are a sinner. Instead of excusing yourself and your sin, consider the bad news of the Christmas story. When you do, the good news becomes more meaningful than tinsel and turkey and stressful shopping. Jesus came to rescue you, forgive you, transform you, and ultimately to deliver you. The baby in the manger carried with Him to earth everything that sinners need, everything we all need. It's only when you admit the need that you will be able to fully celebrate the solution that is Jesus. Not just once a year but throughout your life. Life is full of bad news. Even Christmas is bad news to some. But the opposite of bad news of course is good. The good news is Jesus.

13. INDESCRIBABLE GIFT

How do you choose the right gift? You cannot please all the people all the time but for many it is the thought that counts. The thought is valued far above financial consideration. Do you give gifts purely without thought of anything being returned? If so, do you believe others do too? Or do you panic because someone bought you something and getting something for them hadn't even been on your radar? We are of course concerned about choosing just the right Christmas gifts to give. But have you ever received a gift that was beyond description? What kind of gift would it need to be to really be called "indescribable?" Maybe a gift that is indescribable is one that carries a lot of emotions with it. It was given to you by someone special, and it was a complete surprise when it was given. You'll treasure it always because of the memories it evokes. On the other hand, could it be a gift that you cared so little about that you wouldn't even bother to find words to try to describe it!

Nothing is too good for my family, so a quick search of the internet for some indescribably expensive gifts turned up the following. The "Flowerbomb" 15th Anniversary perfume bottle is opulently adorned in 3D-printed rose gold flowers and thorny branches. At around £2,250 per bottle, it is one of the most expensive fragrances on the market at the time of me writing. It is also among the rarest, with just 15 bottles released. It comes in a lavish case bearing its unique number in rose gold calligraphy, printed by hand. If you like time pieces watch manufacturer, A. Lange & Sohne launched several limited-edition watches to commemorate the 25th anniversary of the brand's revival. The £280,000 Lange 1 Tourbillon Perpetual Calendar 25th Anniversary watch will ensure you are never late again. The 624-part L082.1 self-winding movement with perpetual calendar complication and tourbillon escapement corrects for gravity-induced timekeeping inaccuracies. That description of course means it is not indescribable, though they sound baffling. If you want to buy an experience for a gift look no further than a private 12-hour trip for four aboard the Bloon space pod for £410,00.

Such gifts stagger our imagination, but they are not indescribable. Manufacturers will describe these and regular gifts in such appealing ways to entice you into believing that you simply can't live without them. But every human gift can be described. None of these, of course, compare to something made by your child at school, or a card they made themselves. The joy you express when they give you a pair of socks means more to them than anything money can buy. So, it isn't really the socks that matter.

In 2 Corinthians chapter nine, Paul begins by

writing about human gifts. The church in Corinth is taking up offerings to give to the poverty-stricken Christians in Jerusalem. He commends them for their eagerness to help. He then moves his attention from human gifts to God's gift of sending Jesus to earth for us. And he cannot find words to describe what was done. He can only utter the simple phrase, "Thanks be to God for His indescribable gift." Many have tried to express it in words by various forms. Musicians have composed some of their greatest music on this theme: Handel's "Messiah," Bach's "Christmas Oratorio". The Christmas carols, "Joy to the World," "Silent Night," "O Little Town of Bethlehem," and so many more. They have been sung each year, every year for many years. Poets have written poems about it, painters have painted scenes of it, sculptors have paid tribute in marble and various other materials to Jesus, the incredible gift of God's love. They do well but even then, they do not really encapsulate all that needs to be said.

The apostle Paul calls Jesus "indescribable". How would you describe Jesus? What words would you choose? How do you describe God in flesh, who came down from heaven to walk about on our earth? Isaiah said He would be called Immanuel, "God with us." How do you describe that? What words would you choose? Is a thesaurus enough to offer help? How do you describe that which is spirit when all we have ever known is that which is either physical or material? How do you describe God who has all knowledge when all we have is limited knowledge? How do you describe God who is all powerful? How do you describe the eternal? How do you describe the indescribable?

Paul says that we can't. Words aren't adequate. But many of the wisest men in the world have tried to describe Jesus. The Council of Chalcedon in 451 A.D. attempted it. The greatest theological minds of the time came together & tried to describe Jesus. Here is their description:

"Perfect in Godhead and perfect in manhood. Truly man of a reasonable, rational soul and body. Consubstantial, co-essential with the Father according to the manhood. In all things like unto us without sin. Begotten before all ages of the Father according to the Godhead. And in these latter times for us and for our salvation, born of the virgin Mary and of the mother of God. According to the manhood - one and the same Christ, Son, Lord, only begotten to be acknowledged in two natures. Inconfusedly, unchangeably, indivisibly, inseparably and the distinction of natures being by no means taken away by the union, but rather the property of each nature being preserved."

I hope their description has helped you get your head around who Jesus is. If someone asked you to describe Jesus was that simple enough to remember and repeat? The greatest minds and most extensive vocabularies, the most thoughtful philosophers cannot adequately describe Jesus. Paul called Jesus indescribable because of His purpose in coming to earth and the people he came for. The angels announced to the shepherds, "To you is born this day in the City of David, a Saviour who is Christ the Lord." God knew that our greatest need is not for more wealth, nor better schools, better health, not even a better welfare system. Our greatest need is for a Saviour. Our greatest need is to be saved from hell and permanent separation from God How do you describe that? How do you put into words what God accomplished when He sent His only begotten Son into the world?

Paul says something remarkable in his letter to the Romans. In fact, it is astounding even today. He tells the readers, which includes us, that while we were still sinners, while we were still the enemies of God, Christ died on the cross for us. God gives a gift to us, not because He feels obliged, due to our doing anything wonderful for him but because His love for us is so overwhelming. It's a gift of grace, something we do not deserve. And there are no words adequate to describe God's act of grace towards us in Jesus. When you open your gifts, this Christmas will your life be changed forever? When you receive the gifts that have been purchased for you will this make you different in some way? Will they bring peace or give you hope? Will the cost of the gift determine how grateful you are. Or will you be the same as you were the day before you received them, the way you have always been?

When we accept that Jesus is God and he came to save us from our sin, Jesus, the indescribable gift of God, we will never be the same again because of how He affects our life. We are forgiven our sins. We are adopted into His family becoming His children, able to call Him Father. We are guaranteed citizenship in His kingdom. We receive the gift of His Holy Spirit to live within us. We are also given His peace. Not the peace of the world, but the peace that passes all understanding. We gain hope for a sure and certain future.

I knew I would fail in my attempt to describe Jesus because someone else failed before me and he was better at it. The apostle Paul looked at Jesus and said something along the lines of, I can't describe Him. All I can do is fall on my knees and thank God for His indescribable gift. The gift has a giver, but what use is either, without the gift being received? Have you accepted God's indescribable gift to you?

14. THE HIGH COST
OF A FREE GIFT

It is often said, you may have heard it or even said it yourself, "The best things in life are free."? This usually refers to those intangible things in life that a price cannot be put on. Peace of mind, a moment in time that can never be recaptured but caused joy. Seeing a child take the first step or hearing the first word that really was a word. The operation was a success. So much that can bring, relief, joy, peace or even hope. Money will not make you happy, some people say. The rest of us would like to at least have the chance to see if it is true. Often when a company offers a gift, we still wonder how much it will have cost by the time we achieve claiming that free gift. To buy one and get one free, you still must buy one. A free coffee after you have bought ten if the offer is still in date.

If you attend a church meeting it will not be long before you hear the offer of the gift of salvation. This "free gift" has some mistaken ideas around it, perhaps due to the terms "free" and "gift". The best thing in life is a gift from God, yet a high price was paid for it to be made available and stay in date forever. This shouldn't sound strange, any gift ever given to you had to be bought by someone, didn't it? Such a high price was paid for our salvation from sin many cannot accept that it is free. What we have done is so wrong or so bad there must be a price we have to pay! It follows that some think salvation is earned by the "good works" they do. Such as living life in a particular kind of way, keeping certain rules and regulations. Good behaviour is a must, an exemplary life should be demonstrated, generous giving of time or money or both and faithful attendance at church meetings and studies. Surely something that cost so much must be paid for, made up for, recompensed in some way.

On the other hand, the opposite could be true. Having done something so incredibly wonderful, far more than helping an elderly person across the road, it must be rewarded because of how good we have been. We earnt it! Are we able to tip the scales weighed down by something bad we have done. Can we balance the bad by doing far better to outweigh it? The problem arises when our sin is too bad to accomplish that. At what point is our sin so bad it cannot to be made up for by something good enough?

God in His wisdom sees sin for what it is. Sin is sin. We measure it perhaps by what we perceive are larger or smaller consequences. We do not separate the sinner from the sin, or we label some people as worse than others or better than others by some misguided rule we make up in our own minds. A much simpler system is to admit that we all sin and that's that. Having sinned we need salvation from the punishment of it and it cannot be earned. What price would you ask to make up for it? Salvation is not a reward for something we have done, but a rescue from a helpless situation. What could you possibly do anyway that would be so deserving? Salvation is God's gift to people who are undeserving. It is offered to everyone whilst we were still sinners, living our lives in undeserving ways, we were ungodly, and enemies of the one we were sinning against. Salvation is not offered because we love God but because He loved us. Salvation is offered "freely". But does that mean it does not cost anything? Certainly not, an extremely high price was paid. From John 3:16 we read with great emotion, if we haven't become too familiar with the verse, that it cost God the sacrifice of His only begotten Son who he loves. His love for us meant He did not spare His only beloved Son. It cost Jesus his glory and majesty, which He had with the Father before coming to this world. It cost Him the humiliation of becoming a servant, even to the point of suffering and finally dying for our sins as Paul points out in his letter to the Philippians in chapter two. Read it, take note, and consider how much God gave up just to come down and live on earth.

Though this is a gift that cannot be earned there may be a price to pay for receiving it, notice I said 'for' receiving it not 'to' receive it. The apostle Paul accepted the cost by describing what he had done by being crucified with Christ as he wrote in Galatians chapter two. By dying to self, he gave up his old life of privilege for one of suffering, a life of wealth for one of poverty. No one can accept Christ and His salvation on any less terms than the complete surrender of self to Him. All too often we want to accept Jesus as Saviour, have our sin forgiven, secure eternal life but not have Him as Lord of our lives. The word "lord" is a dirty word these days. Nobody wants to be told what to do by someone they think has no right to do so. Jesus though is acceptable as a friend who is of benefit when it suites us. Yet the two are inseparable. No one can accept Jesus as "Saviour of their soul" without accepting Him as "Lord of their life". Jesus Himself made this clear when He warned His hearers that the cost of discipleship is high. So high that many who were following him and even got fed by him turned and walked away. This happened remarkable just after he had fed five thousand. They witnessed it, tasted the bread and fish, but then said thanks for the food and walked away, because his teaching was too hard to take.

The lordship of Jesus over self, life, and possessions must be acknowledged if we are to know, understand and appreciate Him as Saviour! Jesus commissioned His disciples to preach that in His name a renouncing and turning away from sin is possible in His name. There is no taking away of sin apart from turning away from sin. This involves every aspect of your life. There must be a recognition of what sin is and a sorrow that we allowed ourselves to do things that should not be done. Not only sorrow for the past, that we leave behind in the waters of immersion, but zeal for the future which we now look forward to. Sorrow for how we used to live affects how we will now live into the future. The word for this in the Bible is "repentance" and it is the abandoning of our own selfish ways, to live God's way in obedience and companionship with Him.

Many people assume that it is a matter of "just accepting" Him, "with no strings attached". However, consider the words of Jesus Himself – "if you love me, you will keep my commandments". To "receive Jesus", then, requires a full surrender to the lordship of Christ, and a sincere acceptance of His commandments. That is why the "gift" of salvation, while offered freely, still comes a with high price. Salvation cannot be earned, nor merited, by any number of good deeds. It cost God far more than can be explained. It cost Jesus the agony and shame of the cross. It costs everyone who truly receives it the total submission of self and submitting ourselves to the rightful claims of Jesus on our life. He has the right because of who He is and what He has done. Part of the way led to the manger. The baby Jesus grew up though, to be the man who died on the cross to take away our sin. Jesus has paid the high price to offer you the gift of salvation...are you willing to pay the high price of accepting it?

15. ROYALTIES FOR WORK DONE ONCE

It seems such a long time ago now that I cannot quite recall when I first heard a Christmas song being played in the shops this year. It must have been way back in October. I think there were people muttering that it was far too soon. Well, not for those who wrote, performed, and sang it isn't. It can never be too soon to earn money again from work that was done once.

I was 11 years of age when the group Slade sang "Merry Christmas Everybody" for the first time. In those days the best chance you got to see a group, or a singer was on "Top of the Pops" on a Thursday night. This was a must see as it was revealed who had got to the number one slot in the charts that week. As I recall they battled with Wizard who sang, "I Wish It Could Be Christmas Everyday", for the Christmas number one that year. Do they even have a number one spot these days? With so many different charts now for so many different genres of music I can't keep up. But back then it seemed to be more of an event. Noddy Holder who owns the rights of Slade's song writer, Noddy Holder says it is like winning the lottery every 25th December.

Here is a list I found on the internet, something that didn't exist when many of these were hits for the first time, which is taken from various newspapers and magazines about earnings of Christmas songs. It will no doubt be out of date by the time you read this. These songs were written once and yet the stars have had a pay day every year since. Though the figures may well be out of date they give an idea of how good it is to receive royalties.

Merry Christmas Everybody by Slade £500,000
Fairy Tale of New York by The Pogues £400,000
All I Want for Christmas Is You by Mariah Carey £376,000
White Christmas by Bing Crosby £328,000
Last Christmas by Wham! £300,000
Wonderful Christmastime by Paul McCartney £260,000
Mistletoe and Wine by Cliff Richard £100,000
Stop the Cavalry by Jona Lewie £120,000

If they did not want to, the artists do not really need to work now that the work has been done. In fact, some in the list are no longer with us, someone somewhere though is benefitting from their talent. Can you see where this is going? It came to my mind on reading this information, that we can all benefit from work that has been done once but is good for all people for all time. The writer to the Hebrews says:

"And just as each person is destined to die once and

after that comes judgment, so also Christ was offered once for all time as a sacrifice to take away the sins of many people. He will come again, not to deal with our sins, but to bring salvation to all who are eagerly waiting for him". (Hebrews 9:27)

Faithful people in the days of old waited for the one who was to come and be the Saviour of the world. He arrived in humble circumstances in fulfilment of prophecy. The gospel writer Luke records for us that the baby Jesus grew in wisdom and in stature with God and man. As an adult he freely gave His life on the cross at Calvary to take away our sin. Once and for all time sin has been dealt with for all who will come and follow Him.

What work do we need to do for our sin to be taken away? According to scripture the work has been done. What we need to do is acknowledge the one who did it. Our good deeds and behaviour cannot make up for sin or give us the power not to sin. The good news is that Jesus came to take care of us and our sin. You see the gospel is so much more than a self-help book. Without Christ, we were not merely bad or unchurched. We didn't need a bit of help, a hand up. We were dead. Being dead is a huge problem, it's about as bad as things can get. Dead people can't do anything to help themselves. So, the good news about Jesus really begins with this bad news. "All have sinned", and no one can do anything about their situation before God.

Fortunately, the gospel ends with wonderful news! We begin as people who are spiritually dead because of the penalty and the power of sin, but through Jesus, the spiritually dead are raised to life. The good news we read in the Bible isn't simply a message of how bad people become good; it's the power by which dead people come to life. It's not about Jesus making us a little bit better. The gospel is about our cold, dead hearts starting to beat again by the power of God. When a person turns to Jesus and away from sin, they bury their old life by being immersed in water. Then as they raise up out of the water, having become followers of Jesus, we are now resurrected people brought back to life from the dead. Christ has done for us what we could never do for ourselves.

This is done by faith it is not achieved by doing good works. Those who want to be saved from their sin and its punishment trust in the death, burial, and resurrection of Jesus Christ. In that one-time act God breathes into us new and everlasting life. The gospel is about being resurrected; that comes by trusting in Jesus who died once for all. He did not remain in the grave and because of that which happened in the past, in a moment in time, it is for us a present reality.

It does not end at the instance of your baptism, which is immersion in water. This is a new birth and as such there must now be growth. If you have been baptised it will do you well to think back to it often and be reminded of how it felt at the time. Let it move you to keep committing yourself every day to live for Christ. There's more at stake than what happens in your own life. That's because God raised up His Son to raise up hope in your community through you and then let this hope go out to the nation and into all the world. Such a difference should be made in your own life, that people can't help but see it. What is God doing in you and through you, that will cause people to be astonished and wonder what happened to you.

Consider how people wait in anticipation of finding out what the Christmas number one will be. Usually, the number one is a charity record these days. We need to stir up a far greater anticipation for the coming of Christ, just like had been when his birth was waited for. How will people know He is coming back? It can only be by the difference He has made in the life of those who follow Him. By our lives we can show he is back, he is risen. And let people know the work He did once at the cross will pay royalties even now by them accepting the forgiveness He offers.

Jesus intervenes in the lives of those who are broken hearted, held captive by sin, are prisoners of guilt and enslaved to the pain of the past. He steps into that prison cell of death and declares freedom and life. He turns mourning into joy; he turns despair into praise. God wants to touch your life and use your life to raise up hope.

Isn't it time to let Jesus Christ shine his light of truth and mercy and grace on you? Could you then go back to the place you came from, for the people who know you best to look at you in astonished wonder and say, "What happened to you?" In the end, nothing amplifies the message of Jesus' power and grace more than a person dead in sin, decaying and helpless now pulsing with new life and beauty.

Jesus Christ is the way and the truth and the life, no one can come to the Father except through Him. Therefore, believe in Jesus Christ as the Son of God. Turn from a life lived in a way that does not acknowledge Him as Lord. Hand over control of your life to Him by being immersed. Through baptism you die to self and are then raised to live a new life. Out of appreciation and gratitude we then demonstrate the change with the good deeds that you now do, not to earn salvation but to show you have received His wonderful gift of life.

The work has been done; the debt has been paid. Total it up; £sin, £guilt, £death, £enmity, £strife, and £separation from God. Jesus having completed the work once now calls all people to benefit. Add up the royalties that keep getting paid for that one-time act; £forgiveness, £reconciliation, £peace, £hope which all adds up to eternal life with God. A priceless gift given to us for free by someone who did the work once and for all, why not enjoy the royalties of forgiveness, peace, hope and love.

16. LOSE WEIGHT
FOR CHRISTMAS

I along with many other people always try to lose weight ready for Christmas. Sadly, this is a vain attempt to not feel so bad when the inevitable weight is put back on over the holidays. All I do is get back to where I started or even a little further behind rather than further along.

Paul taught that those who had been buried with Christ in baptism were raised to "walk in newness of life". Not only was baptism the symbol of the end of the old life lived without any regard to God or even in rebellion to Him, but it was also the start of the new life of faithfulness towards God. To enjoy the blessings of faith in God there needs to be continual growth. Losing weight to put it back on again becomes discouraging, bad for your health and is a pointless waste of time. Going back to sin and thinking I can be forgiven later and get back on track once I've had my fun is futile. Following Jesus is not just about attending church meetings, agreeing with a set standard of beliefs, and going through the motions of some ceremonies that may or may not find their foundation in scripture. It is a way of life that includes those things so long as they have meaning behind them that are understood by the whole congregation if you are part of a congregation. It is a complete and utter commitment of the whole of your life, every aspect of it, not something to dip in and out of.

You can measure physical fitness in various ways but how do we determine if we have grown spiritually fit. It is not by answering questions on the Bible correctly, it is not by counting how many prayers you say or signing up to endless verse for the day apps. It is not about how much of the Bible you can memorise. Nor is it ticking off a list of what you have deemed to be good deeds. Many things determine the changes brought about by spiritual growth. Though all those things mentioned may have their place and can be helpful, what we do must result in our growing closer to God. As we do, the more we will trust in Him which will be seen in our relying on Him more and putting less effort in our own strength.

You want to lose weight but buy a pie and chips on the way home from being weighed at the diet club. Your knowledge does not lead to action. You hear a good Bible talk or lesson and think, "I really should change". That's a fascinating fact from the Bible, "I really should start reading it every day". My prayer life is awful, I really should pray more often. But do you? Do you say an apple a day keeps the doctor away but never eat an apple? God is not impressed when we talk a good talk. He weighs our actions, looks at the motives and intents of the heart.

In Hebrews chapter twelve we are told about people who are out of shape because they weigh too much and have become too accustomed to and comfortable with their sin. The problem with most of us is that when we look at ourselves to see if we are spiritually overweight, we use the wrong scales. God's standard of righteousness is not some variable weight that depends on how good your neighbour is. When my neighbour is bad, I look good, when they are good, I must up my game to look better. God's standard of righteousness is unchangeable. It won't matter that we might have lived at least better than our neighbour. Easy to do if they are a terrible criminal! To weigh the right amount in heaven we need help from God. The question is not, "Am I as good as others, but am I as good as God." He created us and He alone has the right to determine what it means to be good. Only He can judge correctly. God looks at the heart we are unable to do that. We are more prone to look at the outward appearance, but God sees beyond that into the very heart. He investigates the motives behind the actions. It is not the good works that we do, but rather the condition of our heart that ultimately matters with God. In Matt 7:19-23, we read about people who did all sorts of good things. They even brag about it, *"Didn't we heal in your name, didn't we cast out demons in your name, didn't we prophesy in your name,"* and Jesus says, *"Depart from me, I never knew you."*

We need to be sure we are being weighed by God's standards. The prophet Samuel was told by God to pick the next king of Israel. He was impressed with some men because they were big and strong, but God refused them. Then the prophet came to David and God told him he was the one. God told Samuel that He looks at the heart not the outward appearance. (1 Samuel 16:7). Jesus said that He was the way the truth and the life, no one could get to heaven without Him. Jesus is the only way we can ever weigh the right amount. He will clothe us with His righteousness. He will take our place on the scales. If anyone steps on the scale without letting Jesus take their place, they will be overweight with sin. We do not want to be sinfully overweight and spiritually underweight. Jesus makes us right. Since God says all our good works are no better than dirty laundry. Without the righteousness of Jesus Christ our lives would not have any weight at all. We are weighed down with the cares of this life. We are distracted and consumed with our possessions. We don't seem to have time for God or time to obey Him, there's too much stuff going on in our lives. We need the cleansing blood of Jesus, or we will have all our sins attached to us and will remain grossly overweight.

I became so unhealthily overweight that according to NHS guidelines I qualified for free entry to a club that could help me. I also at one time was so overweight with sin, that according to scriptural guidelines I qualified to have them washed away for free. Taken out of the world of takeaways, chocolate, and unhealthy habits I was inducted into another world, a club full of people who had the same problem as me. Remarkably, in a similar way I was taken out of the kingdom of darkness which is Satan's world and added to the kingdom of light, the kingdom of God. Having been given books to help me eat more healthily by making better choices, it became apparent owning the books made little difference if they were not read and then acted upon. A dusty Bible is much less use when left as an ornament than it can be. It is so much more than a book, and we need to do so much more than read it. It gives us instruction for all we need for life and godliness.

To help me lose weight there were weekly meetings to see how I was doing. Was I on track? Did I follow the directions given? As that day of the week, we get weighed, rolls around, I am either afraid to get on the scales because I know I haven't done the right thing, Or I face them with joy knowing I have been good. Any opportunity to meet with other followers of Jesus is a joy and a time of encouragement. However, sometimes on a Sunday I face the Lord's supper afraid because I examine myself and I know there have been some failures over the past week. Temper lost, gossip shared, things that I know better not to do. How much better to recognise our faith and life go hand in hand and we are consistent Monday to Saturday with what we sing and pray about on a Sunday.

Nobody knows us better than we do. At the diet club the scales tell the truth. What I have done in secret does become evident, without me shouting about it. People notice when we do as we should with healthy eating habits. If you eat fruit in front of people but go home for fish and chips and a bar of chocolate what you do in secret will become known eventually. The change might be gradual but all at once it seems it will be evident. Is this the way it can be with our Christian life and our habits of discipleship. The light you shine in front of other Christians will fade or get brighter according to the disciplines we practise in private. What do we do with this? Are you overweight with sin? Sin weighs you down, it stops you enjoying life. Some people think if you put God out of your mind you are free then to do what you want. But you are not free. (Romans 6:16) *"Do you not know that if you present yourselves to anyone as obedient slaves, you are slaves of the one whom you obey, either of sin, which leads to death, or of obedience, which leads to righteousness?"*

To have a healthier lifestyle you do not avoid food altogether. You still need to eat. You merely make better choices. Am I now a slave of better choices. Yes, if I want to be heathy. Or I can be a slave of the wrong choices. I am a slave of one or the other, but I need to choose the one that is best. Spiritually you can choose to do your own thing, but you will become a slave to selfishness, pride, and greed. In making your own choice you are choosing to be a slave to sin.

Without food you will die so food is needed but not overindulgence. Some food is to be avoided. The words we speak can be good or bad, encouraging or discouraging, truth or lies. But we need to use words. We can love or hate. The Bible describes the two situations by saying we are either being dark or light, living in the darkness or light. We all start in the same place. If you now want to lose the weight of sin, how do you do it? Recognise that all of us are qualified to be saved because all of us have sinned and fallen short of the glory of God. Understand that it is only Jesus who has the answer because He is the answer.

By dying on the cross at Calvary He rescued us, our salvation from sin is not our work, He has rescued us by giving His life as a ransom to save us from the punishment of our sin. We were kidnapped and held captive by sin. However, the purchase price has been paid. The better choice is Jesus and if we turn from our sin, and to Him He will wash our sins away in the water of our immersion into His name. What a relief to lose all the weight of sin.

17. IT'S A WONDERFUL LIFE!

One of my favourite Christmas films is "It's A Wonderful Life". The basic premise is that George Bailey, is a man who feels trapped in his small hometown. He was going to travel and see the world but before he went his father suffered a stroke, so George had to stay home and run the family-owned bank's affairs. There were difficulties and challenges to overcome. Taking two steps forward and three steps back as problems arose and grew George became desperate until he was ready to take his own life. It was the only escape as far as he could see. However, prayers were offered on his behalf which reached heaven and an angel called Clarence who still needed to earn his wings was sent to help. (This is just a story; I have no biblical reference for that!)

Clarence showed George what life would have been like had he not been born. As a youngster he had saved his little brothers life. Skating on ice his brother fell through it. George became deaf in one ear in the process of saving his drowning brother. This later meant he couldn't join the army which would have enabled him to fulfil his desire to travel. To add insult to injury his brother did enlist and went on to be a war hero saving many lives. It wouldn't have happened if George hadn't saved his life that day on the frozen pond. When a little older he prevented a pharmacist, he worked for, accidently giving a boy poison instead of medicine saving the boy's life and the chemist from whatever repercussions that would have brought. Besides that, when working in the bank, he helped people who couldn't pay their mortgage or rent or who needed money for food and fuel. Allowing them to payback later or at a reduced interest rate. All this is shown to him. By the end of the film the townsfolk rally round and collect enough money to save the bank. If he hadn't been born the world would have been a worse place.

What if Jesus had never been born? What would life be like? How would the world look? It's bad now but how much worse would it be? Christianity would not exist. Hospitals, educational establishments, work against poverty, many institutions based on biblical principles and faith would not have impacted the world for good. Basically, there would be the Law of Moses and the Ten Commandments and on the other hand terrible pagan practices. The world would be a very different place if Jesus had not been born.

We would all be waiting if we had any regard for the scriptures. Of course, we couldn't call them the Old Testament because there wasn't a new one yet. We would all be waiting for a promised Messiah to appear and be wondering of it was ever going to happen. Between the last writings of the Old Testament and the first of the New Testament, 400 years had passed, and people were wondering will it ever happen. What if he hadn't come yet and science was spouting what it now is about evolution and the big bang. Our biggest defence is that Jesus lives. How would we deal with it if he hadn't been born? But Jesus was born, there can be no doubt about that. It is a fact of history. Every time you write the date it speaks of the time Christ was born. The difference that Christ has made is in the fact that he was not only born, but the purpose of his birth was so that he could die as a human for our sake, and he rose again to give us new life. What difference has Jesus made to you?

Jesus came for those who are less than perfect, those who are far from perfect, and those who are anything but perfect. *God made Jesus who had no sin to be sin for us, so that in him we might become the righteousness of God (2 Corinthians 5:21).* You can be like Matthew, the tax collector, who was going about his daily business working for the oppressors of his own people and making good money out of it. Who understood, relinquished, and left behind his past, transforming his future. All Jesus said was "follow me", and he did.

Or you can be like Pharisees and the teachers of the law with their stiff-upper lip, narrow mind set and false self-importance and self-righteousness. You can be like the woman at the well who if she was around today would be a prime candidate for a daytime television discussion show. But having kindness shown to her brought not only her but through her the town to Christ. You can choose to be like Pilate who washed his hands of Jesus even though he could find nothing wrong with him.

Your life can be turned around like Zacchaeus or the woman caught in adultery, or the prostitute who understood who Jesus was and what he was offering. Like them you can be saved from your sin. Make no mistake, you can know you are saved by being obedient to His Word. You are not saved by joining a congregation. You are not saved by a prayer. You are not saved by being sprinkled. You are not saved because your parents are Christians or even because you were born in a Christian country. You are saved because of what Jesus did for you. By having a complete change of heart resulting in you living by and being obedient to the teachings of the Bible because through them you are reconciled to God. So, you believe, you have a change of heart (the Bible calls it repent) you confess that Jesus is Lord of your life and are immersed in water, burying your old life in a watery grave into his death and you raise up out of it into a new life. By doing that you can know you are saved. And your life becomes significant and worth living.

When we take our eyes of Christ we get bogged down with life and ask, "is it worth it?" That is nothing new, it was even dealt with in the Bible.

In Heb. 12:1-3, we read, *"Let us run with endurance the race that is set before us, looking to Jesus, the founder and perfecter of our faith, who for the joy that was set before him endured the cross, despising the shame, and is seated at the right hand of the throne of God. Consider him who endured from sinners such hostility against himself, so that you may not grow weary or fainthearted."*

In our Christian walk, our life with Christ at the centre, we will encounter hardship and hostility, but we must remember that Jesus endured far more than we can ever imagine, and we must use that realisation to strengthen us as we run the race set before us, knowing that if we do not grow weary or fainthearted that we, like Jesus, will receive the joy that is set before us.

Paul expressed this same idea in 2 Corinthians 4:16-17, *"So we do not lose heart. Though our outer nature is wasting away, our inner nature is being renewed day by day. For this slight momentary affliction is preparing for us an eternal weight of glory beyond all comparison."* If life is getting you down and you do not know where to turn or want to give up. It's time to have a change of heart and mind. Focus on Christ and not yourself. Let him give your life new meaning and purpose by dying to your old life and starting anew.

18. NATIVITY BEHIND
THE SCENES.

Here is a true story, it might not seem to be true, it may even seem like a far-fetched fantasy but what I am about to tell you is true.

A great sign appeared in heaven: there was a woman clothed with the sun, with the moon under her feet, and on her head, there was a garland of twelve stars. Being pregnant, she cried out in labour and in pain to give birth. And another sign appeared in heaven: behold, a great, fiery red dragon having seven heads and ten horns, and seven diadems on his heads. His tail drew a third of the stars of heaven and threw them to the earth. And the dragon stood before the woman who was ready to give birth, to devour her Child as soon as it was born. She bore a male Child who was to rule all nations with a rod of iron. And her Child was caught up to God and His throne. Then the woman fled into the wilderness, where she has a place prepared by God, that they should feed her there one thousand two hundred and sixty days. And war broke out in heaven: Michael and his angels fought with the dragon; and the dragon and his angels fought, but they did not prevail, nor was a place found for them in heaven any longer. So, the great dragon was cast out, that serpent of old, called the Devil and Satan, who deceives the whole world; he was cast to the earth, and his angels were cast out with him.

Then I heard a loud voice saying in heaven, "Now salvation, and strength, and the kingdom of our God, and the power of His Christ have come, for the accuser of our brethren, who accused them before our God day and night, has been cast down. And they overcame him by the blood of the Lamb and by the word of their testimony, and they did not love their lives to the death. Therefore rejoice, O heavens, and you who dwell in them! Woe to the inhabitants of the earth and the sea! For the devil has come down to you, having great wrath, because he knows that he has a short time."

Now when the dragon saw that he had been cast to the earth, he persecuted the woman who gave birth to the male *Child*. But the woman was given two wings of a great eagle, that she might fly into the wilderness to her place, where she is nourished for a time and times and half a time, from the presence of the serpent. So, the serpent spewed water out of his mouth like a flood after the woman, that he might cause her to be carried away by the flood. But the earth helped the woman, and the earth opened its mouth and swallowed up the flood which the dragon had spewed out of his mouth. And the dragon was enraged with the woman, and he went to make war with the rest of her offspring, who keep the commandments of God and have the testimony of Jesus Christ.

What did you think about that? Would you believe this is the third account of what we call the nativity. We read the story of the birth of Christ in Matthew and a longer version in Luke. We also have in Revelation chapter twelve an account of what was going on behind the scenes. The real story behind the story as it were. Satan is furious, God has a plan to save humans and somehow this child who is to be born holds the key. If Satan could kill this child, if the dragon could devour the child at birth, then God's plan to save the world would be over before it began. All would be lost, we would be lost, helpless and hopeless in our sin. So, in response to Satan's plans a war broke out to protect the child, why did the child need protecting? This whole war, this battle in heaven took place so that this child could live long enough to be put to death to save you from the gossip you are guilty of, that lie that you told, that dirty thought you had, that burst of anger, this was all for you. All have sinned, no matter how good we are we can never be good enough, we need help.

No wonder the angels rejoiced! They had fought the dragon and saved the child's life. Satan used Herod to try and kill the child, but his plan did not work. The magi went home a different route. Joseph and Mary hid in Egypt. That wicked man Herod however, in serving Satan brought about horror as baby boys were put to death. This is serious. Horrifically serious. These things happened so the plan to save us would be fulfilled. If we had never sinned none of this would be needed. Are we taking our role as God's children seriously?

The war is won, Satan only has a limited time and so he will try and bring us down. Are you fighting him or giving him ammunition? God has done all he can to protect us and bring about our salvation. We have the armour of God. Are you wearing it? Are you using what you have at your disposal to protect yourself from the evil one? Do not engage in sin, when you do you join sides with the one who tried to kill the son of God. You will be on the side of the one responsible for the baby boys dying at the time of Christ's birth. Whose side are you fighting on?

We have this debate. If not with ourselves certainly with others. It is a concern about Christmas. What should we do because the Bible doesn't tell us to celebrate the birth of Christ. What? Really? The angels rejoiced and sang about it. The shepherds celebrated and spread the word. The three or more kings or wise men watched and waited for years then travelled far to see the child at a risk of their own lives. The baby Jesus was saved from Satan; he was protected from Herod. And you don't want to celebrate! Repeatedly reference is made to the prophecies fulfilled at his birth. In Philippians chapter two Paul gives another account of what God did through Jesus in sending him to us in human form. Jesus left heaven and equality with God o live in poverty and danger to save us from our sin and reunite us with God.

Don't let the commercialism, the parties, the presents under the tree, the films, the pop songs, the white Christmas, the turkey, and mince pies get in the way. Do not let Satan use all that to undermine the great victory that was won over him when Christ was born. It occurred to me that maybe this is the way he is trying to hush up his colossal failure to the point we have bought into it. Because of all this commercial stuff we even push aside the prophecy fulfilling miracle that is the birth of Christ which had been planned from the beginning of time. But don't you know we even date our calendar from it.

We do not know the date Christ was born. And though there is no instruction to observe anything at this time, the angels celebrated, they sang as they welcomed his birth. The shepherds celebrated. The Wise men risked their lives to visit him. We spend so much time debating if they were Kings or were wise or how many of them there were we miss something. They had gifts, gold for his Kingship, Frankincense for his divinity and myrrh to symbolize his death. And because of all the wrong stuff about it we miss the reality that God so loved the world he gave his only begotten son. What better time to tell people about it? Even angels and demons cannot separate us from God's love.

Shepherds announced the birth of the lamb who became our shepherd. As he was protected, he now protects us. If you have not accepted Christ as the Shepherd of your life, then who is protecting you? As the angels celebrated Jesus' birth, they will celebrate your new birth if you surrender your life to him today because you will now be under God's protection. Do not be afraid. Confess your belief in Jesus Christ the Son of the living God. Turn from your sin. Be baptised so the angels will have a reason to sing again as they welcome your new birth.

19. A WAY IN A MANGER

Only two gospels, give just a few words to inform us about the birth of Christ. Those few verses tell us of prophecy fulfilled. The world had been made ready by the empires that had gone before and prepared the way for Rome to bring about the ideal time for Christ to arrive. Yet nothing is commanded about how to keep what has come to be called Christmas. Whatever it is you think about it one thing we know for sure is that at a particular time in history something did happen. What was it? Why did it happen? For a summary let me take you back to creation, to the start of the story.

Gen 1:1-2 In the beginning God created the heavens and the earth. The earth was formless and empty, and darkness covered the deep waters. And the Spirit of God was hovering over the surface of the waters. There follows a description of how everything was created culminating in human beings being created and placed in the Garden of Eden. Everything there was available to them, it was all good and it was all theirs. Except for the fruit of one tree, they were not to eat it, but they did. This disobedient act separated them from God. The whole purpose of creation was that God could live in loving fellowship, friendship, relationship with His creation. But now they were separated.

Gen 3:14-15 Then the Lord God said to the serpent, "Because you have done this, you are cursed more than all animals, domestic and wild. You will crawl on your belly, grovelling in the dust as long as you live. And I will cause hostility between you and the woman, and between your offspring and her offspring. He will strike your head, and you will strike his heel." He will strike your head and you will strike his heel. Here is the first prophecy that someone would come and end the separation reuniting us with God our creator. Sent out from the Garden of Eden things got worse. One of Adam and Eve's sons Cain killed his brother Abel out of jealousy. We then read of two distinct family lines one that worships God the other that disregards Him. Till we get to the time of Noah. By then there is only one family out of all the earth that worships God.

Gen 6:5-8 The Lord observed the extent of human wickedness on the earth, and he saw that everything they thought or imagined was consistently and totally evil. So, the Lord was sorry he had ever made them and put them on the earth. It broke his heart. And the Lord said, "I will wipe this human race I have created from the face of the earth. Yes, and I will destroy every living thing—all the people, the large animals, the small animals that scurry along the ground, and even the birds of the sky. I am sorry I ever made them." But Noah found favour with the Lord. The earth was destroyed, Noah's family repopulated the earth, some followed God, some did not. Of the family line that did, we then follow through to Abraham. His family was chosen by God so that the way to salvation and fulfilment of His plan spoken of in Genesis 3:15 could continue.

Gen 12:1-3 The Lord had said to Abram, "Leave your native country, your relatives, and your father's family, and go to the land that I will show you. I will make you into a great nation. I will bless you and make you famous, and you will be a blessing to others. I will bless those who bless you and curse those who treat you with contempt. All the families on earth will be blessed through you." Abraham had a son who he named Isaac which means laughter as he and Sarah laughed on hearing they would have a child. What's impossible with us is possible with God. Isaac had two sons one of which was Jacob who in turn had twelve sons who became the tribes that made up the nation of Israel. Their families moved into Egypt where they grew into a nation. They left Egypt to go back to the land Abraham had been promised. Moses led them and, on the way, they received what we know as the Ten Commandments. The reason was to let God's people know what was pleasing to Him, and they would mark this nation out as different to all the others that surrounded them.

Exodus 19:3-6 Then Moses climbed the mountain to appear before God. The Lord called to him from the mountain and said, "Give these instructions to the family of Jacob; announce it to the descendants of Israel: 'You have seen what I did to the Egyptians. You know how I carried you on eagles' wings and brought you to myself. Now if you will obey me and keep my covenant, you will be my own special treasure from among all the peoples on earth; for all the earth belongs to me. And you will be my kingdom of priests, my holy nation.' This is the message you must give to the people of Israel."

After settling in the land some followed the Lord others did not. The people rebelled against God, they were overrun by other nations, they cried out to the Lord for deliverance, and he raised up a judge to save them. This cycle of behaviour continued for many years. Eventually the people wanted a king. God allowed it but they made a bad choice. Good king Saul went bad, and God chose David to reign after him. There are fourteen generations between Abraham and David. The promised Messiah was to come from David, and we see in Matthew chapter one there will be another fourteen generations from David to the point when the Israelites were taken in captivity to Babylonia. There would then be another fourteen generations from that time to the birth of Christ.

Psalm 110:1 *The Lord said to my Lord, "Sit in the place of honour at my right hand until I humble your enemies, making them a footstool under your feet."*

Matt 22:41-46 *Then, surrounded by the Pharisees,*

Jesus asked them a question: "What do you think about the Messiah? Whose son, is he?" They replied, "He is the son of David." Jesus responded, "Then why does David, speaking under the inspiration of the Spirit, call the Messiah 'my Lord'? For David said, 'The Lord said to my Lord, 'Sit in the place of honour at my right hand until I humble your enemies beneath your feet' Since David called the Messiah 'my Lord,' how can the Messiah be his son?" No one could answer him. And after that, no one dared to ask him any more questions."

What do you think about the Messiah? Whose son, is He? The Jews did not attempt to deny the conclusion of our Lord's question, which was, the Messiah is not only the son of David according to the flesh, but he is the Lord of David according to his Divine nature, they could not deny this. In fact, there was no other way of opposing the argument, except by denying that the prophecy in question related to Christ. However, the prophecy was so fully and so generally understood to belong to the Messiah that they did not attempt to do this; immediately the text says, "No one was able to answer him a word". They were completely nonplussed and confounded.

The Messiah promised in Genesis chapter three and verse fifteen, was preserved from the destruction of the earth through the family of Noah. He was promised again through the line of Abraham, to Isaac then Jacob's family who travelled from the promised land into Egypt. After they had grown into a multitude they went back to the promised land as a nation. There as God's special people they had laws peculiar to themselves so they could tell others about God.

The promise to Abraham and prophecies that followed all point to the town of Bethlehem, David's hometown. The town that David's descendants would have to travel to, to be counted in the census. Once in Royal David's city something did happen. It is rooted in history and the story began in Genesis. Many, many prophecies were fulfilled at that birth in Bethlehem. But remember Abraham was promised all people will be blessed through him. The way in the manger was for all people.

Gal 3:26-29 For you are all children of God through faith in Christ Jesus. And all who have been united with Christ in baptism have put on Christ, like putting on new clothes. There is no longer Jew or Gentile, slave or free, male and female. For you are all one in Christ Jesus. And now that you belong to Christ, you are the true children of Abraham. You are his heirs, and God's promise to Abraham belongs to you. The birth had to take place; God had to become human to end the separation caused by sin.

Galatians 4:4; "But when the right time came, God sent his Son, born of a woman."

1 John 3:8; *"But when people keep on sinning, it shows that they belong to the devil, who has been sinning since the beginning. But the Son of God came to destroy the works of the devil."*

Matthew 1:1; *"This is a record of the ancestors of Jesus the Messiah, a descendant of David and of Abraham."*

story of the Bible is about God wanting to live in loving fellowship with us and doing everything he could to allow it to happen. He in His love and mercy is giving us the choice to accept him or not. From creation to Noah, from Noah to Abraham, from Abraham to David who was from Bethlehem, from David to Jesus born in Bethlehem. Whatever you think about this season, this holiday, whatever your take is on what it seems to have become, something did happen, prophesied ages ago and fulfilled in a place and time in history.

John 3:16 *"For God loved the world so much that he gave his one and only Son, so that everyone who believes in him will not perish but have eternal life. God sent his Son into the world not to judge the world, but to save the world through him."*

ABOUT THE AUTHOR

Mark Hill

 Mark grew up in Loughborough, Leics. Attending the church of Christ there, he was baptised as a teenager. He attended the British Bible School which was in Corby when it was residential. He is now involved with the school as a teacher along with others travelling to teach in congregations around the UK. and teaching online. He now lives in Northampton with his wife Suzanne, and they have three children. He enjoys working with the church there and all that involves, along with preaching in other congregations. He has recently become a Rep with Next Generation for Christ, promoting the "Story of Redemption" films series.

BOOKS BY THIS AUTHOR

40 Day Journal - Prioritising The Promise

One of the great themes found running through the Bible is that of a promise. A promise is something we take lightly these days but God does not. All of His promises are fulfilled. In this journal you will trace from beginning to end the need for the promise, what it means to us and how it is fulfilled. As much as it is good to have goals in life, it is just as important to keep your promises. What better promises could you make than ones that have God in mind that will be of benefit to your own life and well being but also affect the life of others for the good.

Autumn Notebook

An Autumn leaf themed notebook. 6 x 9 inches. 120 lined pages on white paper. Perfect for mum, dad, grandma, grandpa, children, grandchildren. Scribble notes, make plans, write goals or doodle.

Winter Notebook

A lined blank notebook with seasonal Winter theme with a Bible verse on the cover. For mum, dad, children, grandad, grandma. Notes, lists, diary, blog.

RESOURCES

britishbibleschool.com

storyofredemptionfilms.com

Find a church of Christ near you:
churchesofchrist.co.uk

Printed in Great Britain
by Amazon

34212398R10079